ABOUT THE AUTHOR

Irene Willis is a poet, writer and longtime educator who has taught at many schools and colleges. Before she ever published poetry, she co-authored a children's book and two volumes in a major textbook series with her first husband, the late Richard Willis. Years later, with psycho-analyst Arlene Kramer Richards, she co-authored four books for young adults. Her published poems began to appear in the 1970's, but it wasn't until 1995, after she had been awarded a Distinguished Artist fellowship by the New Jersey State Council on the Arts, that her first full-length collection, *They Tell Me You Danced* (University Press of Florida), appeared in print. Since then, she has published three more books of poems: *At the Fortune Café* (Snake Nation Press, 2005,) winner of the Violet Reed Haas Award and nominated for a National Book Award; *Those Flames*, a finalist for the Philip Levine Prize and released by Bay Oak Publishers, Ltd.(2009), and *Reminder* (Word Poetry, 2014). A three-time Pushcart Prize nominee, she has had grants and awards from the New Jersey State Council on the Arts; the Millay Colony for the Arts; the Massachusetts Cultural Council and the Berkshire/Taconic Foundation. The holder of an M.A. and Ph.D. from New York University and M.F.A. in Poetry from New England College, she is Poetry Editor of the web-based *International Psychoanalysis,* where her column "Poetry Monday" appears monthly. She is a member of the Authors' Guild, and an Educator Associate of the International Psycho-analytic Association.

CLIMATE OF OPINION

Sigmund Freud In Poetry

Edited and with an Introduction by

Irene Willis

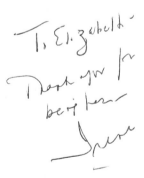

IPBOOKS.net
International Psychoanalytic Books

International Psychoanalytic Books (IPBooks),
30-27 33rd Street, #3R
Astoria, NY 11102
Online at: www.IPBooks.net

Interior book design by Maureen Cutajar, gopublished.com

ISBN: 978-0-9995965-4-8

To: Arlene Kramer Richards and Arnold Richards
and to the memory of my husband,
Bernard Daves Rossell (d. 2016)

"To us he is no more a person
Now, but a whole climate of opinion"
—W.H. Auden

"Everywhere I go I find a poet has been there before me."
—Sigmund Freud

Table of Contents

Introduction

THIS BOOK GREW ORGANICALLY. I read poetry all the time – old books, new books, literary journals – and sometime last year began to notice that many poems mentioned Freud by name. Poetry had always reflected Freudian concepts, of course, but suddenly poets seemed to be more conscious of them. Was Freud having, as they say, "a moment" again? Perhaps. At lunch one day with a couple of psychoanalyst friends, I mentioned this and suggested casually – yes, really casually, just as a topic of conversation, – "Someone ought to do an anthology of poems that mention Freud."

I didn't mean that I should be that someone, but my lunch companions jumped on it.

"Great idea!" one said. "You should do it."

"Me? Why? Shouldn't it be a psychoanalyst?"

"No, *you*. You're the poetry maven," he said, picking at his gluten-free entrée.

So there we were, and here I am, knowing that readers, seeing my name as editor, will be wondering the same thing I did. Why is she the one to do this? Which is why I gave myself such a long – and I hope not self-aggrandizing, these days when we're all newly conscious of narcissism – "About the Editor" at the beginning of this book. How I feel about it now is happy and proud. I love the cover; it's blue, the color of memory, the way it should be, and there's that wonderful picture of old Siggie himself, pen aloft instead of a cigar. Sometimes a pen is just a pen, yes? Because I'm not a psychoanalyst, I can be a bit irreverent, as I'm sure our eclectic readers will understand.

One of my encouragers said, "Why not make it, not just about Freud himself but also about psychoanalysis?"

I thought about that a bit, and so the anthology of poems about Freud morphed into an anthology about Freud, psychoanalysis and, ultimately, about Freudian concepts. Did it become a little too top-heavy with dreams? Possibly. But, as the great man himself said, "Dreams are the royal road to the unconscious."

What fun this has been – and what a lot of work, except for the first part, gathering the poems, and for the next part, arranging them in an order that made some kind of metaphorical sense (don't ask me what that means, my unconscious talking perhaps to yours, as poet Kate Light says (page 47). The rest of it was burdensome detail, much of which was handled by the amazingly competent Tamar Schwartz, Managing Editor of IPBooks, who undertook to secure permissions for the work of poets I do not know personally, who were most of the dead ones. Believe it or not, one of the greatest dead ones, W.H. Auden, I did know somewhat personally. I met him in the 1950's when I was undergraduate chair of a college lecture series, introduced him from the stage, handled publicity for his appearance, and as part of my job, took him to dinner at the White Inn in Fredonia, New York – *alone*, as no one from the English department seemed to have been available, to the amazement of my current poet friends when I tell this story now. He was already wrinkled, as he looks in so many of his pictures, and we had a good conversation, talking at length, as I recall, about current affairs and specifically about Charlie Chaplin, someone I brought up who was much in the news then, with one sort of scandal or another. Auden was warm and cordial, signing a photo as I asked, with my green-ink fountain pen, a photo I sold a few years ago to a rare book dealer, along with a copy of the introduction typed on my old Royal portable. His lecture was just that – a lecture, and not a poetry reading, which no one there seemed to have heard of then – and I remember one thing from it. "A poet," he said, "is someone who likes to hang around words."

The longer I thought about this project, the more I thought my whole life had been leading up to it. What I didn't remember to discuss with my lunch companions was the fact that I began reading Freud when I was twelve years old.

I checked out his *Basic Writings* from the Bloomingdale Branch of the New York City Public Library on the upper West Side because I thought it would help me explain my budding self to my mother. It didn't. In fact, years later, when she was in her eighties with a group of senior citizens, I heard her ask another woman, "What do you think of these teen-*agers*?" as if adolescence were some newly discovered phenomenon.

How do I feel now that the book is done? Happy and proud. Soon after that initial discussion, one of those friends suggested I apply for a grant to support the project, which I did, with the happy result that we received funding from the American Psychoanalytic Foundation. Their generous support includes amounts for the editor, the publisher and all of those who have given us permission to use their poems. As I said to them in the proposal, it is our hope that the book will be read not only by general readers and people in the field, but also by students of psychoanalysis, who should find much material in the poems for classroom discussion. I know, having been a teacher of literature and composition for so much of my life, I would have a field day with these poems in the classroom. What a treasure trove we have here! (And what a mixed metaphor!)

The poems didn't come just from my first harvest, which was mostly from already published books and journals. After that gathering, I sent out a call to some poet friends, who forwarded it to others, and then to a couple of membership lists that I was part of. Later Duotrope (which I had not heard of) and a couple of other lists of which were also previously unknown to me, picked up the call, and submissions came flooding in. My post office mailbox was full each time I showed up, with poems from all over the world – so many, in fact, that I was forced to decline even some quite good ones. It was a surprise to me, although it shouldn't have been, that so many were from psychoanalysts themselves. But most were from well-published poets, with impressive academic as well as poetry credentials, as you will see in the Contributors' notes at the end of this book. What you will also see is how eclectic a gathering we have, with famous names interspersed among the lesser-known. I tried to select the best, and hope you will agree that this process has made for an absorbing, interesting read. Fittingly, of course, the anthology opens with Auden's famous "To Sigmund Freud," the poem which gave us our title and explains that, no, the great man is not just having a moment. He's part of the way we think now. Whether you're reading this poem for the first time, or re-reading it, I think you will agree with what Auden says in this stanza:

For one who'd lived among enemies so long:
If often he was wrong, and, at times, absurd,
To us he is no more a person
Now, but a whole climate of opinion

This is followed by another famous poem, "The Master," by H.D. (Hilda Doolittle), who was an early patient of Freud's, having sought him out, as I understand, to deal with her bisexuality and who, as you will see in the poem, was ambivalent not only about that but about him. What he did do for her, and for us, was to encourage her poetry.

It won't shock psychoanalysts but general readers may be surprised to learn that his own daughter, Anna, was also one of his patients. A couple of her poems are also included here (pages 23, 25) I don't want to distract you from the pleasure of discovering the rest of the poems by yourselves, except to call your attention to a couple of the earliest irreverent ones, Philip Larkin's witty "This Be the Verse" (page 37) and Dorothy Parker's sonnet, "The Passionate Freudian to His Love." (pages 35–36).

One of the best parts, for me, of this project, was not only gathering the poems but the background reading I did while getting ready for the first harvest. In the process I acquired copies of many fascinating articles and a whole shelf of books about this man who, in my own thinking now, is more important than ever. More about that in the Afterword. As they often say in restaurants before you pick up your fork, "Enjoy!"

W. H. Auden

For Sigmund Freud
(d. Sept. 1939)

When there are so many we shall have to mourn,
When grief has been made so public, and exposed
  To the critique of a whole epoch
  The frailty of our conscience and anguish,

Of whom shall we speak? For every day they die
Among us, those who were doing us some good,
  And knew it was never enough but
  Hoped to improve a little by living.

Such was this doctor: still at eighty he wished
To think of our life from whose unruliness
  So many plausible young futures
  With threats or flattery ask obedience,

But his wish was denied him; he closed his eyes
Upon that last picture, common to us all
  Of problems like relatives standing
  Puzzled and jealous about our dying.

For about him till the very end were still
Those he had studied, the nervous and the nights,
  And shades that still waited to enter
  The bright circle of his recognition

Turned elsewhere with their disappointment, as he
Was taken away from his old interest
    To go back to the earth in London,
    An important Jew who died in exile.

Only Hate was happy, hoping to augment
His practice, and his shabby clientele
    That think they can be cured by killing
    And covering their gardens with ashes.

They are still alive, but in a world he changed
Simply by looking back with no false regrets;
    All he did was to remember
    Like the old and be honest like children.

He wasn't clever at all; he merely told
the unhappy Present to recite the Past
    Like a poetry lesson till sooner
    Or later it faltered at the line where

Long ago the accusations had begun,
And suddenly knew by whom it had been judged,
    How rich life had been and how silly,
    And was life-forgiven and more humble.

Able to approach the Future as a friend
Without a wardrobe of excuses, without
    A set mask of rectitude or an
    Embarrassing over-familiar gesture.

No wonder the ancient cultures of conceit
In his technique of unsettlement foresaw
    The fall of princes, the collapse of
    Their lucrative patterns of frustration.

If he succeeded, why, the Generalised Life
Would become impossible, the monolith
    Of State be broken and prevented
    The co-operation of avengers.

Of course they called on God; but he went his way
Down among the lost people like Dante, down
    To the stinking fosse where the injured
    Lead the ugly life of the rejected,

And showed us what evil is: not, as we thought,
Deeds that must be punished, but our lack of faith,
    Our dishonest mood of denial,
    The concupiscence of the oppressor.

And if something of the autocratic pose,
The parental strictness he distrusted, still
    Clung to his utterance and features,
    It was a protective imitation.

For one who'd lived among enemies so long:
If often he was wrong and, at times, absurd,
    To us he is no more a person
    Now, but a whole climate of opinion

Under whom we conduct our differing lives:
Like weather he can only hinder or help,
    The proud can still be proud but find it
    A little harder, the tyrant tries

To make him do but doesn't care for him much:
He quietly surrounds all our habits of growth;
    He extends, till the tired in even
    The remotest most miserable duchy

Are aware of the change in their bones and cheered;
And the child, unlucky in his little State,
    Some hearth where freedom is excluded,
    A hive whose honey is fear and worry,

Feels calmer now and somehow assured of escape,
While, as they lie in the grass of our neglect,
    So many long-forgotten objects
    Revealed by his undiscouraged shining

Are returned to us and made precious again;
Games we had thought we must stop as we grew up,
    Little noises we dared not laugh at,
    Faces we made when no one was looking.

But he wishes us more than this: to be free
Is often to be lonely: he would unite
    The unequal moieties fractured
    By our own well-meaning sense of justice.

Would restore to the larger the wit and will
The smaller possesses but can only use
    For arid disputes, would give back to
    The son the mother's richness of feeling:

But he would have us remember most of all
To be enthusiastic over the night,
    Not only for the sense of wonder
    It alone can give, but also

Because it needs our love. For with sad eyes
Its delectable creatures look up and beg
    Us dumbly to ask them to follow;
    They are exiles who long for the future

That lies in our power; they too would rejoice
If allowed to serve enlightenment like him,
    Even to bear our cry of 'Judas',
    As he did and all must bear who serve it.

Our rational voice is dumb; over a grave
The Household of impulse mourns one dearly loved:
    Sad is Eros, builder of cities,
    And weeping anarchic Aphrodite.

The Master

I

He was very beautiful,
the old man,
and I knew wisdom,
I found measureless truth
in his words,
his command
was final;

(how did he understand?)

when I travelled to Miletus
to get wisdom,
I left all else behind,
I fasted,
I worked late,
rose early;
whether I wore simple garments
or intricate
nothing was lost,
each vestment had meaning,
"every gesture is wisdom,"
he taught;
"nothing is lost,"
he said;

I went late to bed
or early,
I caught the dream
and rose dreaming,
and we wrought philosophy on the dream content,
I was content;

nothing was lost
for God is all
and the dream is God;
only to us,
to us
is small wisdom,
but great enough
to know God everywhere;

O he was fair,
even when I flung his words in his teeth,
he said,
"I will soon be dead
I must learn from the young";

his tyranny was absolute,
for I had to love him then,
I had to recognize that he was beyond all-men,
nearer to God
(he was so old)
I had to claim
pardon,
which he granted
with his old head
so wise,
so beautiful

with his mouth so young
and his eyes-

O God,
let there be some surprise in heaven for him,
for no one but you could devise
anything suitable
for him,
so beautiful.

II

I don't know what to suggest,
I can hardly suggest things to God
who with a nod
says, "rise Olympos,
sink into the sea,
O Pelion,
Ossia,
be still";

I do not know what to say to God,
for the hills
answer his nod,
and the sea
when he tells his daughter,
white Mother

of green
leaves
and green rills
and silver,
to still
tempest
or send peace
and surcease of peril
when a mountain has spit fire:

I did not know how to differentiate
between volcanic desire,
anemones like embers
and purple fire
of violets
like red heat,
and the cold

silver
of her feet:

I had two loves separate;
God who loves all mountains,
alone knew why
and understood
and told the old man
to explain

the impossible,

which he did.

III

What can God give the old man,
who made this possible?

for a woman
breathes fire
and is cold,
and woman sheds snow from ankles
and is warm;
white heat
melts into snow-flake

and violets
turn to pure amethysts,
water-clear:

no,
I did not falter,
I saw the whole miracle,
I knew that the old man made this tenable,
but how could he have foreseen
the impossible?

how could he have known
how each gesture of this dancer
would be hieratic?
words were scrawled on papyrus,
words were written most carefully,
each word was separate
yet each word led to another word,
and the whole made a rhythym
in the air,
till now unguessed at,
unknown.

IV

I was angry at the old man,
I wanted an answer,
a neat answer,
when I argued and said, "well, tell me,
you will soon be dead,
the secret lies with you,"
he said,
"you are a poet";

I do not wish to be treated like a child, a weakling,
so I said,
(I was angry)
"you can not last forever,
the fire of wisdom dies with you,
I have travelled far to Miletus,
you can not stay long now with us,
I came for an answer";

I was angry with the old man
with his talk of the man-strength,
I was angry with his mystery, his mysteries,
I argued till day-break;

O, it was late,
and God will forgive me, my anger,
but I could not accept it.
I could not accept from wisdom
what love taught,
woman is perfect.

V

She is a woman,
yet beyond woman,
yet in woman,
her feet are the delicate pulse of the narcissus bud,
pushing from earth
(ah, where is your man-strength?)
her arms are the waving of the young
male,
tentative,
reaching out
that first evening
alone in a forest;
she is woman,
her thighs are frail yet strong,
she leaps from rock to rock
(it was only a small circle for her dance)

and the hills dance,

she conjures the hills;
"rhododendrons
awake,"
her feet
pulse,
the rhododendrons
wake
there is purple flower
between her marble, her birch-tree white
thighs,
or there is a red flower,

there is a rose flower
parted wide,

as her limbs fling wide in dance
ecstatic
Aphrodite,

there is a frail lavender flower
hidden in grass;

O God, what is it,
this flower
that in itself had power over the whole earth?
for she needs no man,
herself
is that dart and pulse of the male,
hands, feet, thighs,
herself perfect.

VI

Let the old man lie in the earth
(he has troubled men's thought long enough)
let the old man die,
let the old man be of the earth
he is earth,
Father,
O beloved
you are the earth,
he is the earth, Saturn, wisdom,
rock, (O his bones are hard, he is strong, that old man)
let him create a new earth,
and from the rocks of this re-birth
the whole world
must suffer,
only we
who are free,

may foretell,
may prophesy,
he,
(it is he the old man
who will bring a new world to birth)
it is he,
it is he
who already has formed a new earth.

VII

He will trouble the thoughts of men
yet for many an aeon,
they will travel far and wide,
they will discuss all his written words,
his pen will be sacred
they will build a temple
and keep all his sacred writings safe,
and men will come
and men will quarrel
but he will be safe;

they will found temples in his name,
his fame
will be so great
that anyone who has known him
will also be hailed as master,
seer,
interpreter;

only I,
I will escape.

VIII

And it was he himself, he who set me free
to prophesy,

he did not say
"stay,
my disciple,"
he did not say,
"write,
each word I say is sacred,"
he did not say, "teach"
he did not say,
"heal
or seal
documents in my name,"

he was rather casual,
"we won't argue about that"
(he said)
"you are a poet."

IX

So I went forth
blinded a little with the sort of terrible tears
that won't fall;
I said good-bye
and saw his old head
as he turned,
as he left the room
leaving me alone
with all his old trophies,
the marbles, the vases, the stone Sphynx,
the old, old jars from Egypt;
he left me alone with these things
and his old back was bowed;

O God,
those tears didn't come,
how could they?
I went away,
I said
"I won't have this tyranny
of an old man
he is too old,
I will die,
if I love him;

I can not love him
he is too near
too precious to God."

X

But one does not forget him
who makes all things feasible,
one does not forgive him
who makes God-in-all
possible,
for that is unbearable.

XI

Now I can bear even God,
for a woman's laughter
prophesies
happiness:

(not man, not men,
only one, the old man,
sacred to God);

no man will be present in those mysteries,
yet all men will kneel,
no man will be potent,
important,
yet all men will feel
what it is to be a woman,
will yearn,
burn,
turn from easy pleasure
to hardship
of the spirit,

men will see how long they have been blind,
poor men
poor man-kind
how long
how long
this thought of the man-pulse has tricked them,
has weakened them,
shall see woman,
perfect.

XII

And they did;
I was not the only one that cried
madly,
madly,
we were together,
we were one;

we were together
we were one;
sun-worshippers,

we flung
as one voice
our cry
Rhodocleia;

Rhodocleia,
near to the sun,
we did not say
"pity us,"
we did not say, "look at us,"
we cried,
"O heart of the sun
rhododendron,
Rhodocleia,
we are unworthy your beauty,
you are near beauty the sun,
you are that Lord become woman."

Thoughts of a Young Girl

Note: These untitled notes were shared by a poetry blogger who discovered them while reading a biography of Sigmund Freud. Young Anna wrote:

"for one hour, one day, I do so wish
to be rid of myself, no longer to know
my own face, my own poor hands,
just once not to feel my thoughts.
that man, that drayman, would I be,
his shoulder rubbed sore from the strap;
that porter, his neck bent, burdened;
someone other, who has no need to cover up,
as I have been doing for so long,
with satisfactions cleverly calculated,
yet so stingy, so pitiful, that the dog
sunning himself in the corner there
would never look up from his bone for them ......*!!!*

ps: -it's the mask we keep on wearing all day .... and
one day this pretence take away the real self we were born
with*!!!!!*

Wolf

According to an article in the *London Guardian*, in the mid-1920's, Freud's then 30-year-old daughter Anna became the owner of Wolf, "a magnificent and intelligent German Shepherd," with whom Freud fell in love. On each of her father's birthdays thereafter, Anna would present him with a poem, which she would attach to the dog's collar before sending him in to see her father. Here is one such poem:

On account of the coming of much of the clan
A house ban
Now 'gainst his normal demeanor and noise
Silently poised.
His love for the friendly as edible
As with sucked-up thermometers, immeasurable.
Thus kept from the banquet so nourishing and fair
He gets from the table scraps none of his share,
Unwavering true: 'spite of fleeting pleasure's bite,
He withdraws, quite dog-like.

Exhibit of Freud's Neurological Drawings and Diagrams of the Mind
(New York Academy of Medicine, May 2006)

Faded sketches of eel genitalia
he drew when a student of twenty,
still wedded to what he could know
through a microscope, reproducing
their cells, labeling them with tiny letters –
pea-shaped on tangled strands
to map the testicles he couldn't find,
embedded past the eye's penetration.
Then, lacking means to measure further,
he uncoupled himself from proof
and launched into shadows.
Case after case studied on the couch,
conceiving what he couldn't see –
ego and id intuited, sketches of the mind.

Freud Town

Devil say I am an unlocated.
Window of myself devil.
Say nobody sit.
There nobody light.
The lamp devil.
Say one glimpse of it.
From outside do the trick do.
The trick devil.
Say smell this devil say.
Raw bones devil say the mind.
Is an alien guest I say.
Devil outlived devil in.

Elizabeth Anne Socolow

Freud and the Others in the Old Days

About suffering they were never wrong, the old masters. . .
          W. H. Auden, "Au Musée des Beaux Arts"

I think from the time I knew about Beethoven being deaf,
I measured genius in part by the degree of suffering
any one of them had to endure. Jungle fever and dysentery,
storms at sea for the explorers like Humboldt,

ridicule and the enmity of the upright and religious for Galileo and
so many of them, but Newton lost his father before he was born
and his mother to a step-father when he was four.
I always knew, I think, he imagined the pull between

distant bodies because he was sent away
to live with his uncle when he was still very young,
and bonding being so unreliable, he never married.
At a certain age, that was the worst sacrifice I could imagine:

my mother threatened me with spinsterhood
as the ultimate punishment all my life in her home
and in that fear, I was like many girls of my time, and
did not feel so hurt or different that I wanted to chase down

talk therapy, or an analyst. I cannot recall when I stopped
comparing them—Darwin against Freud, Mozart against
Shakespeare. Or even why I began. I remember, though,
a conversation with a close friend on the subway when I was

31

sixteen or seventeen about the material of study: what
difference did *that* make? Marie Curie gave herself radiation
poisoning which seemed a terrible consequence of curiosity
and ambition—we had already learned from studying

Achilles in the Iliad it was not worth giving up long life
to have enduring fame and glory. But Freud: he just took
ordinary things, families, houses, hugs good night in the dark
and from our daily lives, he told amazing stories the Greeks

knew first. That seemed to me astonishing, nothing special
like uranium to start from, and yet he saw something
altogether new, like quilts stitched from bits of garments, or
girl's dresses made of patterned flour sacking in the old days.

Freudiana

i.   II

...we are all ill, i.e., neurotic...—Sigmund Freud

All ill, some very, some not so much or not
so evidently—though perhaps for that
all the more ill. Overall I'd say I was ill,
but not quite ill all over as there's still
some small patch of well, a windowsill
of the psyche I can look out from
and see how much more ill you are than I am.

ii.   Royal

Dreams are the royal road to the unconscious.—Sigmund Freud

A royal road, a ragged road,
a ruffian, raffish, rascal road,
I dreamt a road the royals ran
between their various castles and
the barracks where their guards abode.
We run this road the royals roared
because this road is ours not yours,
it's ours because it was decreed
this road be called the royal road.
It wasn't called the public street

nor was it called the common way;
it wasn't paved for common feet,
and if you want to pass you pay
with coins whose heads are royal heads,
whose tails wear plumes of royalty.

The road was ours since time began
and time is also ours not yours,
for as we hardly need to say
it was decreed that hours should be,
that hours and years and eras be
prerogatives of royalty.

The Passionate Freudian to His Love

Only name the day, and we'll fly away
In the face of old traditions,
To a sheltered spot, by the world forgot,
Where we'll park our inhibitions.
Come and gaze in eyes where the lovelight lies
As it psychoanalyzes,
And when once you glean what your fantasies mean
Life will hold no more surprises.
When you've told your love what you're thinking of
Things will be much more informal;
Through a sunlit land we'll go hand-in-hand,
Drifting gently back to normal.

While the pale moon gleams, we will dream sweet dreams,
And I'll win your admiration,
For it's only fair to admit I'm there
With a mean interpretation.
In the sunrise glow we will whisper low
Of the scenes our dreams have painted,
And when you're advised what they symbolized
We'll begin to feel acquainted.
So we'll gaily float in a slumber boat
Where subconscious waves dash wildly;
In the stars' soft light, we will say good-night—
And "good-night!" will put it mildly.

Our desires shall be from repressions free—
As it's only right to treat them.
To your ego's whims I will sing sweet hymns,
And *ad libido* repeat them.

With your hand in mine, idly we'll recline
Amid bowers of neuroses,
While the sun seeks rest in the great red west
We will sit and match psychoses.
So come dwell a while on that distant isle
In the brilliant tropical weather;
Where a Freud in need is a Freud indeed,
We'll always be Jung together.

Philip Larkin

This Be the Verse

They fuck you up, your mum and dad.
 They may not mean to, but they do.
They fill you with the faults they had
 And add some extra, just for you.

But they were fucked up in their turn
 By fools in old-style hats and coats,
Who half the time were soppy-stern
 And half at one another's throats.

Man hands on misery to man.
 It deepens like a coastal shelf.
Get out as early as you can,
 And don't have any kids yourself.

They Loom Large, Parents

I remember especially my father's fears and his tears
because they were so terrible, and so rare.
Tears for the days he came home, gray, and said,
every time, the first metaphor I ultimately understood:
another candle has gone out.

I thought until I was about five he only meant that
something he had tried to do had not worked out.
And from birthdays, I thought perhaps he had not had time
to make a wish before a candle flame guttered. I do not remember
when I first really understood
one of his patients had died.

He complained when I was six or seven that, as a cardiologist, he was in
a profession with the ultimate adversary.
He could not win the war he said (after we had defeated
the Nazis) but only some skirmishes. I had to figure out
that an 'adversary' was an 'enemy' and he meant *death*.

Sometimes he saved lives, but often he could not. Later, when it
was clear to him that my little sister was schizophrenic,
he became terrified of Freudian analysis. He believed in brain disease,
and took her to therapists who agreed with him that,
until drugs could alter brain chemistry, we would get *nowheremuch*
with psychosis.

He raged at Freud who only looked, my father said,
at ordinary families who could afford to have sons overly attached
to mothers or fathers to daughters. He wanted something new
for the extremes, for the abnormal brain, damaged at birth if not
in birth, and he hated labeling our situation in a fixed way.

He kept tropical fish and a small garden and he was fond of saying to me:
For your sister, there is one thing to be hoped,
a great mystery. The late bloomer.

Family: Attempted Speech
For Amy

A family of no conversation
alternating monologues and silence

at times shouts and blows
someone hitting her head against the apartment wall

as her own mother did
which she so hated

we loved each other only through our pores
what to do with this love we could not conceivably say

so family is a way of demonstrating
how incomplete we are while belonging to each other

like tires of an armored car we can never drive
artichoke leaves around a hairy heart

dear sister let us tell this open secret
let us wave the painfully specific dented kitchen spoons

take the canned peaches from the dusty shelf
listen to the radiator knock

let the story flow like milk
to a nursing woman's breasts

let it open like the door
to the crying room

Love Duck

My father, through his tears beseeches me to write a poem
about Mother and me going out for Chinese food without him.
Frankly, I'm suspicious. I think he wants to know what exactly
we were doing in his absence. Did we dine face-to-face? Sit side-
by-side in a plush banquette? Did we toast with Mai Tai's
or lean mutually over to sip from a Scorpion Bowl arrayed
with seahorses and native dancers, while twirling tiny parasols
and laughing? What actually transpired at Shun Lee East?
Mother and I discussed the latest productions of Gurney
and Mamet, the Johns' retrospective, the new non-fiction
by Tracey Kidder. I listened to her merciless opinion on
installation art invading Chelsea and tried to convince her
she shouldn't be concerned that the Knicks starting five
are swathed in seaweed-dark tattoos as long as they're still
winning, nor hastily dismiss *The Sopranos* for their non-stop
use of expletives. In his anguish, he needs to believe that we
were *close.* So I don't mention how amidst our gastronomic
pleasure, she couldn't help scorning this, excoriating that
or how the copious libations pacified those suppers, and
the fact that she'd insist on paying. I inform him only that
his absence enabled us to celebrate our lust for Beijing Duck:
the crackling skin, the slightly gamy meat, the scallions crisp,
the ooze of night-sky plum sauce, pancakes warm and soft
in their lacquered dragon box. The doting wait-staff, grease-
less spring rolls, those dumplings with an aromatic broth
concealed inside. Near perfection amidst ambivalence

we'd never fully overcome. We'd start with bone-in spare ribs.
Like a brute, I'd gnaw the marrow and much to her chagrin.
At moments, I'd notice other twosomes middle-aged and
older at nearby tables, who'd occasionally glance at us
and might've felt, perhaps with envy, perhaps with pleasure:
here sits a mother and a son who purely adore each other.

Freud

Come to think of it, I never speak of Mom
much now, though I go on and on about Dad.
My generation's given "Mom" a beating,
I think: there's no son who hasn't got his gun
out for the old dear—the dear in the headlights!
Think it could be, like, you know, like…*Freud*?

Speaking of beatings, who's taken more than Freud,
lately? From the belly of "The Beast," not Mom's:
Shtand ze kike against zer vall! Aim ze headlights…
But why beat Freud instead of dear old Dad?
Dad's the one who's always pulling out his gun,
longing to give *someone* a "Christian" beating!

Freud got a few things wrong—that's worth a beating?
Let's whack some Christians instead of poor Freud.
It's clear they understand about "The Gun"—
but what about "The Cave"? No, no, not Mom's—
and let's not even go there about Dad's.
Their *zeitgeist* is a scramble toward headlights—

figures projected on a wall by headlights—
then, once there, instituting someone's beating.
How do you break it to your "real-life" Dad

that twenty centuries of this *schadenfreude*
are too much? That this smokescreen called "Mom"
just hides the cave of God-Our-Daddy's gun?

They co-opt Jesus into their hired gun—
that rabble-rousing Jewish kid, with head lice—
then claim he cut this strange deal with *his* Mom?
And he'll *return*—to give the sons a beating?
No wonder we're devouring poor old Freud!
We'll swallow any tale "revealed" by "Dad."

"I can sell you *anything!*" My own dad
points his shaking finger like a gun
at me. He wonders who the hell is Freud;
he winks and elbows me about "headlights."
His diaper leaks. His pride takes a beating.
I shoo him off to Florida with "Mom."

Amerika: a graveyard, a Mom-and-Dad
beating. Whistle past. Switch on your headlights.
A gun can *be* a gun, even for Freud.

Your Unconscious Speaks to My Unconscious

Your unconscious speaks to my unconscious
like subtitles of another language, saying:
Why? Why did you do this
to me? So while we are laughing and playing,
my unconscious, hearing, says, *What did I*
do? Now ours is crying, weeping, saying,
Why are you doing this? Why
do you leave me? Aren't you staying?
and mine, astonished, says, *Sweetheart, I*
am right here. I am here. Your eyes
looking into mine. Your fingers in my hair.
But as our spines bend, something unties
in me, and I *am* no longer there.
For I have already watched you go,
in the movie, in the darkness, through the snow.

Halloween

Your ghost ate chocolates and refused to ski.
Mine drank music and wore boots.
Yours loved to shop, to pot furious bowls.
Mine finally removed his red toupee

Our ghosts dance on the shaggy Greek rug
between us.
We'll fold their sheets, top and bottom,
to make our beds.

William Coombes

A Child's Life Sentence

You talk too much, and what you say sounds foolish.
Do as I say, not as I do.
Your nose is too big for your face.
Your legs are crooked.
You have wide feet, like a duck.
You might turn out to be a half decent swimmer.
How many times do you have to be told children are to be seen but
    not heard?
You look the most like the man who gave you away.
Read your Bible.
No you can't have any comic books.
Comic books come from the devil.
Stop your crying.
If you don't stop your bloody crying, I will give you something to
    really cry about.
Eat your supper.
Don't tell me you don't like turnips.
There are children starving to death in this world you know.
Carry your Bible to school.
Be a good witness for Jesus.
Don't worry about the teasing.
You'll be storing up riches in heaven.
You want to go to heaven don't you?

"Thoughts are tyrants that return again and again to torment us."[1]

The days turned into weeks, into months, into years that seemed to
   be the same one after the other.
Like the awkward limping tick of a broken clock, *Eye* couldn' t wait to
   grow up.

[1] Emily Bronte, *Wuthering Heights*.

Stones In Shoes on the Shoreline of Dark Lake

"No one cares about your thoughts, or your life," a relative scolded.

"You have to be a celebrity, an authority, before anyone will read what you have to say," the Pentecostal preacher exclaimed. "You will never go anywhere in life! People like you, who think too much, eventually end up a corpse in a ditch of suicide! It is too bad God didn't get hold of you before your life was ruined. You should pray, asking God for a healing of your mind."

In senior years now, the sound of *Eye's* deceased adopted father's voice still echoing in his ears, "You will never amount to much of anything."

As a result, *Eye* has wondered all these years if anyone ever does amount to much. In the scope of an entire life, what exactly is there to amount to; the most financially wealthy corpse; the best looking dead person; the one who told the most lies; the person who lobbied for, and maintained popularity their entire life; the control freak, who strategically dominated every one they said they loved?

The man *Eye* grew up calling Dad, in frustration used to ask, "What is the matter with your head?" Being a boy, not a medical doctor, the only answer *Eye* could ever give was, "I don't know."

Now, *Eye* looks back thinking all their words were lies. Statements of mean-spiritedness and symbols of attempted crucifixions like a crown of thorns placed upon his head. *Eye* shrugs them off, like old worn out hats. Watches them fall onto the page.

And the shoes? *Eye* kicked them off. Observing their scuffmarks, threw them into Dark Lake. Watched the splash and ripples upon the water of the canvas surface.

"We must take sides. Neutrality helps the oppressor, never the victim. Silence encourages the tormentor, never the tormented."[1]

One day *Eye* will die too. His voice will be silent. All that will remain are these songs of existence. They will be what they are.

[1] Elie Wiesel.

Speculations about "I"

A certain doubleness, by which I can stand as remote from myself as from another.

> —*Henry David Thoreau*

I

I didn't choose the word—
it came pouring out of my throat
like the water inside a drowned man.
I didn't even push on my stomach.
I just lay there, dead (like he told me)

& "I" came out.
(I'm sorry, Father.
"I" wasn't my fault.)

II

(How did "I" feel?)

Felt almost alive
when I'd get in, like the Trojan horse.

I'd sit on the bench
(I didn't look out of the eyeholes
so I wouldn't see the carnage).

55

III

(Is "I" speaking another language?)

I said, "I" is dangerous.
But at the time I couldn't tell
which one of us was speaking.

IV

(Why "I"?)

"I" was the closest I could get to the
one I loved (who I believe was
smothered in her playpen).

Perhaps she gave birth
To "I" before she died.

V

I deny "I,"
& the closer
I get, the more
"I " keeps receding.

VI

I found "I"
in the bulrushes
raised by a dirtiness
beyond imagination.

I loved "I" like a stinky bed.

While I hid in a sentence
with a bunch of other words.

VII

(What is "I"?)

A transmission through space?
A dismemberment of the spirit?

More like opening the chest &
throwing the heart out with the gizzards.

VIII

(Translation)

Years later "I" came back
wanting to be known.

Like the unspeakable
name of God, I tried

my 2 letters, leaving
the "O" for breath,

like in the Bible,
missing.

IX

I am not the "I"
in my poems. "I"
is the net I try to pull me in with.

X

I try to talk
With "I," but "I" doesn't trust
me. "I" says I am
slippery by nature.

XI

I made "I" do
what I wasn't supposed to do,
what I didn't want to do—
defend me,
stand as an example,
stand in for what I was hiding.

I treated "I" as if
"I" wasn't human.

XII

They say that what I write
belongs to me, that it is my true
experience. They think it validates
my endurance.
But why pretend?
"I" is a kind of terminal survival.

XIII

I didn't promise
"I" anything & in that way
"I" is the one I was most
true to.

Nostalgia

It challenges our inner boundaries
to crack and leak a little…
Memories that were nothing
more than mere fine times,
anchor themselves to strands
of imaginary light, awaiting gloss
to mirror the moon's sheen.
Time hammers with age,
chipping the mind spaces
where latent memories linger,
unchecked, crawling the dark.
Here, they grow buoyant,
plump with expectation,
fizzing, floating to the forefront,
only to be beaten back by
a haemorrhaging mind,
accepting the truth of things.
Orbs burst, grainy ashes,
a sobering warning.
We need a celestial hunter in the void
who can cut the Gordian knot
to purge the fakers in hiding,
screen memories Freud called them.
Outside the self, the world dims to grey.

Accused

In January, the day of my last appointment,
I left my umbrella on a seat on a Red Line train,
its cloth, mostly separated from the spokes,
but held in places by small threads;
enough to cover part of a person in a storm.

That last day I sat with you,
surrounded by your collection of clocks, fish,
huge leafy plants, reptiles,
and the silent presence of Horton the owl,
I thought the office was not clean.
You mentioned a new law against keeping birds as pets.

Half my life I made the pilgrimage there,
revealing my dreams,
leading my life under your direction.

I called you the morning in April I read about you
in the paper.
"Accused psychiatrist gives up his license."
"But what I did was long ago," you tell me.
Redemption?

I see now,
your obsession with clocks.
Each time I saw you there were more:
clock sculptures, high tech clocks,
antique pocket watches,
clocks that chime, tick and talk.
Time will tell,
you must have known.
And the creatures you keep who know,
instinctually,
not to grow too big for their aquariums,

and the owl,
tethered to a pole, his white and black droppings
a putrid pile on the newspapered floor.

Why did I think this jungle was a refuge?

When I found myself standing on a Cambridge street,
in the rain, with no umbrella,
I thought about the limitations of such devices;
the way they turn inside out in the wind.

Emily Berry

Freud's Beautiful Things

A cento

I have some sad news for you
I am but a symbol, a shadow cast on paper
If only you knew how things look within me at the moment
Trees covered in white blossom
The remains of my physical self
Do you really find my appearance so attractive?
Darling, I have been telling an awful lot of lies lately
If only I knew what you are doing now?
Standing in the garden and gazing out into the deserted street?
Not a mermaid, but a lovely human being
The whole thing reminds me of the man trying to rescue a birdcage
      from the burning house
(I feel compelled to express myself poetically)
I am not normally a hunter of relics, but...
It was this childhood scene...
(My mother...)
All the while I kept thinking: *her face has such a wild look*
... as though she had never existed
The fact is I have not yet seen her in daylight
Distance must remain distance
A few proud buildings; your lovely photograph
I find this loss very hard to bear
The bells are ringing, I don't quite know why

What makes all autobiographies worthless is, after all, their mendacity
Yesterday and today have been bad days
This oceanic feeling, continuous inner monologues
I said, "All the beautiful things I still have to say will have to remain
     unsaid," and the writing table flooded

Misery and Frustration
—for M.S.

They say one part of wisdom
Is learning to let go when you have to.
But if you give up your good drinking buddies
Misery and frustration, you wonder
What else might drop from the picture.
There is this problem with recovery
You'd like to mention to your therapist,
If you could find the right moment, because
The group somehow doesn't seem to touch it.
Will your sex life go blank like a movie screen
After the feature, your brain
Lapse from keen, your art depart
Like Anthony's gods? Surely a man should worry?
Then there's the issue of brutality.
You hate to be mean. Misery and frustration
Were loyal pals for years; don't you owe them?

Yes, but remember your gardening arts and skills
Have taught you how to be kind to tendrils.
Unwind them cautiously. You can tell
They're living things by their tensile grip.
What you can't tell is that they're parasites,
Thieves and killers. Well, that's nature for you—
Everyone organism for itself.

Do not burn them.
Carry them off to the forest,
Which will slowly eat them.
Misery and frustration are delicious,
They'll make good mulch, you'll see them join

What Wordsworth called the life of things,
Those porous layers, though it may take years.
Meanwhile invent a ritual farewell.
In the men's sweat house one unstated aim
Is to extrude the bitter juice of grief
While gravely regarding one's own genitals
And watching others too, scanning their scars,
Until the heat becomes intolerable
And the heart threatens to stop.
I know a woman who buried her uterus
After her hysterectomy, and said prayers for it,
Although rabbis advised her this would be lawless.
At least you've learned to cry, at least there's that.
Meanwhile—look at your hands
Starting to sprout.

They say another part of wisdom
Is opening, letting things enter, making welcome
As to festival—come on, unbutton her, unloose the stubborn
Doors from their jambs—
But that's a knowledge you already know.

Thelonious Monk

for Michael Thomas

A record store on Wabash was where
I bought my first album. I was a freshman
in college and played the record in my room

over and over. I was caught by how he took
the musical phrase and seemed to find a new
way out, the next note was never the note

you thought would turn up and yet seemed
correct. Surprise in ′*Round Midnight*
or *Sweet and lovely*. I bought the album

for Mulligan but stayed for Monk. I was
eighteen and between my present and future
was a wall so big that not even sunlight

crossed over. I felt surrounded by all
I couldn't do, as if my hopes to write,
to love, to have children, even to exist

with slight contentment were like ghosts
with the faces found on Japanese masks:
sheer mockery! I would sit on the carpet

and listen to Monk twist the scale into kinks
and curlicues. The gooseneck lamp on my desk
had a blue bulb which I thought artistic and

tinted the stacks of unread books: if Thomas
Mann depressed me, Freud depressed me more.
It seemed that Monk played with sticks attached

to his fingertips as he careened through the tune,
counting unlike any metronome. He was exotic,
his playing was hypnotic. I wish I could say

that hearing him I grabbed my pack and soldiered
forward. Not quite. It was the surprise I liked,
the discordance and fretful change of beat.

As in *Straight No Chaser*, where he hammers together
a papier-mâché skyscraper, then pops seagulls
with golf balls. Racket, racket, but all of it

music. What Monk banged out was the conviction
of innumerable directions. Years later
I felt he'd been blueprint, map and education:

no streets, we bushwhacked through the underbrush;
not timid, why open your mouth if not to shout?
not scared, the only road lay straight in front;

not polite, the notes themselves were sneak attacks;
not quiet—look, can't you see the sky will soon
collapse and we must keep dancing till it cracks?

Tom Daley

Mass for Shut-Ins

Look, the eye is lazy
and the cars outside
rumble the floorboards.

I haven't opened the windows
in weeks except to dislodge
the ice from the roof and gutters.

The air fills with a subtle tinnitus
packed with the rustle of freon
from the refrigerator.

There, ghosts from half-listened to
recorded books settle
into the collapsing plush

of the air that scours
the inside of my ears. The scratch
of the pen on the gridded pad

relaxes into a semi-sour
resentment over tomorrow's
tasks. New glasses a definite

imperative. Change the bank
accounts to *Payable on Death*.
Find out what the Freudians

mean by object-oriented.
Deface your attention deficit.
The pilot of that German plane—

what was he breathing into?

Laurel Blossom

No Is the Answer, the Answer Is No

Then your shoulder or your head or your whole body
collides with a wall of bricks, the pain
so dazzling the remotest memories of your childhood
flare up like faces

when a match is struck in the dark, a glimpse
of your own quick shadow on the cave wall
and all the names you call out to come back, come back
hollow, the smell of sulphur on their breath, or else

a door open and you rush in, so surprised
by your forward momentum you wince
to find yourself intact and standing
in the room you wanted so badly to stand in—

empty, bare white, no windows, no secrets,
two doors and a ladderback chair with a rush seat
planted in the middle of the floor. *This is your life.*
It makes you want to throw up. The door

back to where you came from stands open, darkness
not in your face, somebody laughing, a whole history of failure
you'd really rather not recall in this story.
Do you know who that voice is? Old flame

Mr. Muse, Sinatra-smooth, two cigarettes in an ashtray
burning, tempting you
to confuse the messenger with the message
it takes a lifetime

to translate into usable language. Shoot.
Take a shit. Take voice. Take flying lessons.
Say slough of despond twice with a straight face.
Write rhymed verse

so accessible it makes you suspect
among poets and petlovers alike. Relax
in the lonely chair your father left you,
the needlepoint chair handed down to you by your mother,

the crooked chair Van Gogh painted of himself
when he was almost happy. These are your instruments
of torture and deliverance, your Book of Kells, the skeleton
key in the heart-shaped lock. Twist it

however you like, it opens: you cannot escape
your freedom. That second door might still, don't you think,
lead to an absolutely sunstruck patio, fragrant mountains
by the sea, red geraniums—look!, the light

is bulging at the door,
longing to engulf you and carry you away
to *heaven, I'm in heaven*, like poor old, dear old
dead Fred Astaire, dancing up and down the rungs of his chair.

Laura Sheahen

Minotaur

It was hard to find
the psychiatrist's office

so many false corners
so many locked doors

the lone candle long gone

but I did reach the room
hanging with meat

the doctor deservedly
covered in blood and drippings

he fled
I stretched out on the shredded couch

that was when
the maze began

Jill Stein

When I Was Six My Father Had the Power

There in the evening heat
in that tropical hum
the mean dogs gathered in a semi-circle
snarling at the small black one
who swung his head from left to right
as if he might discover
somebody who pitied him.
And I begged my father who still had the power
to erase all sorrows
to save him from the rest.
And he, knowing he still had this power
and treasuring it like a secret silver star
locked next to his heart
leaped into the fray
with a stick and a stone
until the mean dogs turned and ran
down the empty road
like a viscous clot of badness
washing away. And my mother,
her face contorted, whirled around to me
and asked how I could send my gentle father
into danger, my good father
who could not say no to me

and I grew mangy along my back,
my teeth lengthened and I knew
I was the evilest of those dogs,
and the blood of the gentlest one
dripped from my lips.

Irene Willis

Always the Man Somewhere

1

Always the man is somewhere
other than where
I am.
When I am in Paris he is in London.
When I am in London
he is in New York.
When I am on the East Coast
he is on the West.
Always
somewhere
delivering non-messages
keeping mailboxes empty
snowing the channel
making static on the line.

2

That he is somewhere
that his voice plays its tape in my head
keeps me from seeing
the man beside me at the counter
or the next table
on the plane seat
or the bed.

3

Always the man somewhere
the man I cannot say good-by to
the man I am always saying
good-by to.

4

Carefully he looks at me.
From the side of his eye
he looks at me
weighing the possibilities.
I sense him there
and weigh the possibilities
after he leaves.
When it is too late
I try to call him back
but he has been temporarily
disconnected.

Odysseus, His Homecoming

So this was the way
the Goddess answered prayer –

the greying stranger
by their marriage-bed

his spattered hand
outstretched for hers

which for years had only
woven broken threads?

Jean Hollander

"And they shall wear purple. . ."

In your dream you tell me
I'm dressed in lilac,
like the bush that won't bloom
in our garden,
while neighbors luxuriate
in groves of fragrance.

When I was thirteen
I sewed myself a dress of lilac
out of old curtains—
layers of lilac lace-trimmed fabric
descended and flowed
from my shoulders.

A lady at a bus stop
praised it: "Lovely."
Mother distracted—
we missed our bus,
had to wait for half an hour:
"You and your dress!"

The guilt of purple:
Color of my soul.

Juditha Dowd

Viewing Manet's Olympia *with My Granddaughter*

The room invites. Passing through green damask drapes
we meet a servant bringing flowers from an admirer.
But look at the courtesan on her bed, her confrontational gaze.
Short and less voluptuous than a classic nude—thin
is more indecent, wrote Manet's friend Baudelaire.

You're fifteen, in early bloom. Olympia, perhaps a few years older.
Orchid tucked behind an ear, a countenance reminding us a little
of a singer … Miley Cyrus or Madonna?
One hand clasps an ivory shawl, the other guards her wares.

Between us, an easy silence.
I try to remember fifteen and how I might have thought,
stop myself from telling you that girls like this had little choice,
for you must already know—sex today more forthright
(yet from what I can tell, still fraught).

I say, See how he's made one eye larger, the tense line
of her mouth—she's not expecting *us*.
You wonder why, unclothed, she'd bother with jewelry.

Six decades separate us, much history. But if art's task is seduction,
by now we may have both become the body here for hire.
I cross my legs, dangle a satin slipper, recall the mosaic of desire.
You finger the ribbon knotted at your throat.

And These Are My Fears

Jellyfish, the slap of their spectral tentacles,
their circle closing.

And my sister no longer there to save me.

Heights, sometimes, a fear that developed later.
Paralysis. Blindness.

Fire. The loss of my possessions,
which I care about too much.

I fear how my heart
counts on being aflame.

I am younger than everyone –

when you die, oh my loves, any one of you,
I am afraid I will not be able to stop crying,
as sometimes happens in dreams.

What will I do when there is no waking?

I fear the loss of touch. I'll clutch
at the wheel, turn too hard.

On Waking after Dreaming of Raoul

If Freud was right and dreams of falling are
dreams of having fallen then you must have been
the beautiful declivity of that hill, Raoul,
the speed was so seductive and the brakes so
unreliable, and so intricate and so abstract
that when I touched them they squeaked like a jar lid
coming loose and I was embarrassed, but not sad,
at being the one flat wheel that bumped down the hill
in an unsteady gulp of denial—oh no oh no oh no—
until I woke up chilly, damp, my breath unsteady.

In order to recover I sit at the desk studying the Order
of the Holy Ghost Retreat and Old Age Home
until dusk comes down the street elm by elm, here
where they've managed to cure them with a tincture
so poisonous the leaves, though living, are frail
and blanched. I think of you, Ruby Fiori's
half-brother, a thief, and a cook.
Because what good is it any more, pretending
I didn't love you; after all these years you must
be jailed or dead, and it is a relief to give up
reticence which as you once said is merely
impetuosity held tightly in check.

Over the gold swells of sunset lawns the old
men come rolling in their iron chairs, pushed
around by nuns, their open mouths are *Os*
of permanent dismay. Far away the stars are
a fine talcum dusting my mother's one good black
dress, those nights she gunned the Desoto
around Aunt Ada's bed of asters while you shortened

the laces of my breath. Despite the nuns, despite
my mother and my own notions of how bad girls
end up educated and alone, the door opens and you
walk in, naked, you, narrow and white
as the fishing knife's pearl handle, and you kiss me
until my resolve grows as empty as the dress
from which I step, both brave and willful.
I love you, although I didn't know it yet,
anymore than these old men on the dole
of some nun's affectionate disdain
knew that they would end up poor,
mortgaged to a ghost, and living in a place like this.

Alicia Ostriker

Insomnia

But it's really fear you want to talk about
and cannot find the words
so you jeer at yourself

you call yourself a coward
you wake at 2 a.m. thinking *failure,*
fool, unable to sleep, *unable to sleep*

buzzing away on your mattress with two pillows
and a quilt, *they call them comforters,*
which implies that comfort can be bought

and paid for, to help with the fear, the failure
your two walnut chests of drawers snicker, the bookshelves mourn
the art on the walls pities you, the man himself beside you

asleep smelling like mushrooms and moss is a comfort
but never enough, never, the ceiling fixture lightless
velvet drapes hiding the window

traffic noise like a vicious animal
on the loose somewhere out there—
you brag to friends you won't mind death only dying

what a liar you are—
all the other fears, of rejection, of physical pain,
of losing your mind, of losing your eyes,

they are all part of *this!*
Pawprints of *this!* Hair snarls in your comb
this glowing clock the single light in the room

Humidifier

—*After Robert Pinsky*

Defier of closed space, such as the head, opener
Of the sealed passageways, so that
Sunlight might entering the nose can once again

Exit the ear, vaporizer, mist machine, whose
Soft hiss sounds like another human being

But less erratic, more stable, or, if not like a human being,
Carried by one, by my mother to the sick chamber
Of my childhood—as Freud said,

Why are you always sick, Louise? His cigar
Confusing mist with smoke, interfering
With healing—Embodied

Summoner of these ghosts, white plastic tub with your elegant
Clear tub, the water sanitized by boiling,
Sterile, odorless,

In my mother's absence
Run by me, the one machine

I understand: what
Would life be if we could not buy
Objects to care for us

And bear them home, away from the druggists' pity,
If we could not carry in our own arms
Alms, alchemy, to the safety of our bedrooms,
If there were no more

Sounds in the night, continuous
Hush, hush of warm steam, not
Like human breath though regular, if there were nothing in the world

More hopeful than the self,
Soothing it, wishing it well.

After Ravensbruck: The Woman from Holland Speaks to Me in a Dream

The dream is the liberation of the spirit.
                              —Sigmund Freud

Out of the coal-black
she moved toward me. She limped and was very old.
Wallpaper backdrop curled like rolled dollar bills.

"I traveled the world with
my story, false wall in my bedroom—
the rationed cards."

Waved her sister's locket in mid-air. Suddenly
it hung about her own thin neck.

"There is no pit so deep—yet
He is not deeper still," she nodded.

She held up a worn leather bound-book.

"Carried it into the barracks. Like a stolen scrap of bread.
The She Wolf of the SS,—
Angels distracted her."

She took a deep breath. "Lice were our friends,
read *Psalms* one-match-at-a-time." She paused. Then
circled me. Her wrinkled hands cupped my hands—

Asked what I will do with the rest of my life.

In memory of Corrie Ten Boom (1892-1983)

Merridawn Duckler

Earth Room

In sleep I feared my soul would divide,
range free, having shrugged off the body,
go down to my basement where I once slept walked as a child,
our official childhood photographs, tilted a nail's width.

My feet glided like that to the Earth Room,
behind a nondescript door in Soho where an angel sat
at a desk & pointed to the sign: *no pictures,*
for aren't angels always pointing at something

and forbidding you to take them? The dirt was undulant, pure black,
verdant, like Walter de Maria's hair, filled a former galley
packed in since 1977 for me and this other guy
to gaze at in awe and when I turned away I saw

him wave to a man across the street in a window,
just transferring things from box to box,
exactly how my feet moved in sleep walk
all hoard and squander crushed like thyme under each sole.

You aren't supposed to wake sleepwalkers, moving toward
their sure destination, for the soul is shameless about orders.
That dirt was dark as cake. Since the artist forbid reproduction
I took a memory instead of you, love, smiling under a great stair.

Vasiliki Katsarou

Terrarium

Once
she thought
she saw
a soul in miniature

a bonsai
magnified inside
a glass terrarium

the flowering tree
and the One
wielding the ax

as the tree grows
so
it hones the ax

The Sword in the Stone

My analyst looked up briefly.
Naturally I couldn't see him
but I had learned, in our years together,
to intuit these movements. As usual,
he refused to acknowledge
whether or not I was right. My ingenuity versus
his evasiveness: our little game.

At such moments, I felt the analysis
was flourishing: it seemed to bring out in me
a sly vivaciousness I was
inclined to repress. My analyst's
indifference to my performances
was now immensely soothing. An intimacy

had grown up between us
like a forest around a castle.

The blinds were closed. Vacillating
bars of light advanced across the carpeting.
Through a small strip above the windowsill,
I saw the outside world.

All this time I had the giddy sensation
of floating above my life. Far away

that life occurred. But was it
still occurring: that was the question.

Late summer: the light was fading.
Escaped shreds flickered over the potted plants.

The analysis was in its seventh year.
I had begun to draw again—
modest little sketches, occasional
three-dimensional constructs
modeled on functional objects—

And yet, the analysis required
much of my time. From what
was this time deducted: that
was also the question.

I lay, watching the window,
long intervals of silence alternating
with somewhat listless ruminations
and rhetorical questions—

My analyst, I felt, was watching me.
So in my imagination, a mother stares at her sleeping child,
forgiveness preceding understanding.

Or, more likely, so my brother must have gazed at me—
perhaps the silence between us prefigured
this silence, in which everything that remained unspoken
was somehow shared. It seemed a mystery.

Then the hour was over.

I descended as I had ascended;
the doorman opened the door.

The mild weather of the day had held.
Above the shops, striped awnings had unfurled
protecting the fruit.

Restaurants, shops, kiosks
with late newspapers and cigarettes.
The insides grew brighter
as the outside grew darker.

Perhaps the drugs were working?
At some point, the streetlights came on.

I felt, suddenly, a sense of cameras beginning to turn;
I was aware of movement around me, my fellow beings
driven by a mindless fetish for action—

How deeply I resisted this!
It seemed to me shallow and false, or perhaps
partial and false—
whereas truth—well, truth as I saw it
was expressed as stillness.

I walked awhile, staring into the windows of the galleries—
my friends had become famous.

I could hear the river in the background,
from which came the smell of oblivion
interlaced with potted herbs from the restaurants—

I had arranged to join an old acquaintance for dinner.
There he was at our accustomed table;
the wine was poured; he was engaged with the waiter,
discussing the lamb.

As usual, a small argument erupted over dinner, ostensibly
concerning aesthetics. It was allowed to pass.

Outside, the bridge glittered.
Cars rushed back and forth, the river
glittered back, imitating the bridge. Nature
reflecting art: something to that effect.
My friend found the image potent.

He was a writer. His many novels, at the time,
were much praised. One was much like another.
And yet his complacency disguised suffering
as perhaps my suffering disguised complacency.
We had known each other many years.

Once again, I had accused him of laziness.
Once again, he flung the word back—
He raised his glass and turned it upside-down.
This is your purity, he said,
this is your perfectionism—
The glass was empty; it left no mark on the tablecloth.

The wine had gone to my head.
I walked home slowly, brooding, a little drunk.
The wine had gone to my head, or was it
the night itself, the sweetness at the end of summer?

It is the critics, he said,
the critics have the ideas. We artists
(he included me)—we artists
are just children at our games.

First Time Reading Freud

My copy of his *Introductory Lectures*
had an odor I couldn't place, an organic,
vaguely fleshy…pulpy…baby wipes-
type smell-though not exactly. At 18
I was having trouble concentrating,
though the words, according to theory
were processing themselves in my unconscious
while I kept track of girls in miniskirts
wafting in and out of Olin Library
like wide-winged tropical birds. I'd glance down
at Freud's bleak head floating on the cover,
half in stark shadows, monocle in place,
then gaze across the room at a Korean beauty
whose virtually flat face had gotten her
some modeling jobs, and covers of her own.
She promised her mother she'd wear pantyhose
every day, to help her keep out the boys—
as if we'd get inside by accident.
I put my nose to Freud, bent the spine back
deeper to smell…an infant's soft moist head?
…a mother's breast dusted with talc?

I learned about the promise to her mother
when I pointed to new packages of hose
stacked tall on a chair by her bed.
I don't know how I got into her room
or how Freud's language crept into my head—
superego, pleasure principle,
displacement, latent and manifest,

and all the ugly Oedipus business—
babies with sex and murder on the brain,
little Viennese girls hard-wired
to admire their first glimpse of *something egstra,*
yet why hadn't I touched mine till I was 16,

and why did our professor have to tell us
about the woman he saw at Woodstock
lifting her naked baby to manipulate
his penis in her mouth, both mother
and son *cooing,* he said, with pleasure?
Does anybody see a problem here?
he asked an amphitheater full of freshman.
Manipulate was the very he used. Spackling
putty—that's what that book smelled like.

Mario Lopez

Mario Lopez is standing outside
    the Ed Sullivan theater
    at one o'clock on Friday.
    He's filming some segment
    for Extra or Access Hollywood
    or some other show like that.

Mario Lopez is surrounded by women:
    there are women standing behind him
    as part of the background shot
    and then over on the street
    many more women congregate
    to watch Mario Lopez do his thing,
    to appreciate his dimples, his pectorals,
    his abs, his power, his fame, some
    men are there too but mostly women.

At the therapist's office I sit on the couch and say,
    "I would like to be the Mario Lopez
    of poetry."

"What does that mean?" he asks.

"It means I would like to be surrounded
        by women wherever I go," I explain,
        "I want women following me
        to the grocery store, to the dry cleaners,
        to the library, on the subway,
        everywhere I want women wanting me."

"That doesn't have much to do with poetry,"
        observes the therapist,
        "sounds to me like you want to be loved."

"Yeah yeah," I say, and so the session begins,
        we talk of desire, parental neglect,
        conditional affection, while downstairs
        in the pet store the hamster runs on its wheel,
        getting nowhere.

He runs and runs and runs, chasing after
        some unattainable goal, until at last
        he's wiped out and, still breathing heavily,
        sits on the side of his cage, nibbles a carrot,
        feels a little bit lighter and more free.

So too does the therapy help me:
        at the end of my forty-five minutes,
        dashing o'er hurdles of anxiety
        and besting the marathon of self-doubt,
        I feel – for a moment! – content
        to seek love not from strangers, but within.

Walking back to work, I cannot believe that
    Mario Lopez is still outside
    the Ed Sullivan theater!
    How long does it take to film a segment?!
    He's still surrounded by women,
    but now he's starting to sweat –
    flubs another line, curses quietly.
    "Let's do it again," says the director.
    The women cluster closer. Lopez squirms.
    He looks about as happy as I look
    when I am filing papers at my desk,
    which is to say, *it's a job.*

Suddenly I feel great pity
    for Mario Lopez: dimpled Adonis,
    Latin demigod whom no bell can save
    from the endless weight of the world's
    too-too-much idolatry. Strange duality;
    how wonderful and hard his life must be.

How lucky I feel to be so free
    and utterly unknown,
    writing poems that are not poems,
    stopping into the supermarket
    on my way back to work,
    observed by absolutely no one,
    purchasing a perfectly ripe plum,
    crunching into the purple-red skin,
    letting the juice run happily down my chin.

Said the Poet to the Analyst

My business is words. Words are like labels,
or coins, or better, like swarming bees.
I confess I am only broken by the sources of things;
as if words were counted like dead bees in the attic,
unbuckled from their yellow eyes and their dry wings.
I must always forget how one word is able to pick
out another, to manner another, until I have got
something I might have said . . .
but did not.

Your business is watching my words. But I
admit nothing. I work with my best, for instance,
when I can write my praise for a nickel machine,
that one night in Nevada: telling how the magic jackpot
came clacking three bells out, over the lucky screen.

But if you should say this is something it is not,
then I grow weak, remembering how my hands felt funny
and ridiculous and crowded with all
the believing money.

Creative Listening

Ask again. You ask. Again you find silence.
You give up. You wait, and the silence deepens.
Now is then. As if you were meant to suffer
eternal rejection.

Someone now will hear if you dare to whisper.
Someone now is holding silence within her.
Someone now has tuned her third ear to your voice.
Do you hear her listen?

The First Dream

is the dream of greed, abundance, warm and wet and soft, so plentiful it almost smothers you. Baskets of candy underneath the bridge, uncounted unnamed treasure, glittering.

Next is the dream of fear, the witch moves in next door, steals all your plenty, that thing chasing you has half a face, your feet are welded to the ground. Tornadoes roar, black as the world. You fall.

The dream of failure, you stand up before your class wearing a flannel nightgown and you've never read the book, don't know the students, then you see the school board lined up in the back, their eyes avid on you.

The dream of hope.

The dream of colors, a low yellow house, the jade-green lake that lights your face as you cross in your cobalt boat beneath star-salted midnight sky.

The dream of dailiness, you wake to the alarm, shower and dress, eat breakfast, leave for school, go through the first two classes, the alarm goes off, you wake, shower and dress …

The dream of sex, Sean Connery/James Bond and you outwit the spies, keep giddy balance as you run along the ridge pole, and it all ends right, just you and James, just you.

The dream of tenderness.

The dream of loneliness, out on a naked road, you walk a crimson field littered with alabaster statues, perfect noiselessness.

The dream of loss, your child was kidnapped, tortured, your grandchild run down by a truck: why did you put her bed out on the road?

The dream of being lost, you can't find home, you come down off a scaffold to an unfamiliar lake, the tunnel has no end. What is the way? Now lives depend on you, room after room is added to the old bick school you have to scurry through, you're running out of time.

The dream of death.

The Encoder

A woman at the desk gives me some forms.
Questions I cannot answer well.
Have I experienced pressured speech?
I answer no while in the throes of it.
The psychiatrist is practiced in code.
I try to tell him everything. I mean
all of it. He listens well and gently
tries to give me tools and levers
and a place to stand like Archimedes.
I can't tell him about the strange
gold writing. Not yet, I don't know
when I'll know him well enough.
He keeps so much hidden; he is
a still pond, opaque with lilies.
How I would like to write
in gold after the rain stops. I used
to love the rain; now, I can barely
go outside. Thunder makes me
restless, lightning inspires me
to make letters on a page, jagged
mountains and blue clouds.
When I sit in his coral chair, the one
with the arms that hug you, the masks
begin to peel off. His too, I think,

though he quickly withdraws
like the arroyo waterfall. Some codes,
some slogans. He writes down
what I say and don't say. I don't
believe as he believes. He saved me.
He hears poetry down to the bone.
I know because he exhaled sharply
at that killer last line, the one that did
me in, that slayed me and him both.

Freud's War

A cento

I became a therapist against my will
A strange feeling of forlornness, a feeling I could not have stood
Painful isolation, quite steep and slanting
A beautiful forest which had the one drawback of seeming never to
     end
I have had to struggle so long
I have always been frank with you, haven't I?
I wanted to explain the reason for my inaccessibility
I am lying here on a short leash in this filthy hole
So far I haven't been locked up
Several people point to gaps in my face where the little girl has been
     cut out
She screams and screams without any self-control
Ravaged by the heat and the blood-&-thunder melodrama
Neither describable nor bearable
I felt I had known her all my life

Freud

I am old, often ill, and only work for 5 hours with students and patients. There isn't a long waiting list anymore, clients in need of help prefer younger people. Until recently my fee was $25 an hour; as a result of the general impoverishment, I have lowered this to $20 or $15 . . . some of my adult children are out work and have to be assisted or supported.

—Sigmund Freud, age 76, answering a request for analysis

I never imagined you so frail, reduced
to seeing patients for less than the fee
at a mental health center. No, my image
comes from bronze statues analysts display
on their shelves, from Studies in Hysteria,
and a mid-life photograph taken when
your hair was dark and your trimmed beard
had turned gray. You wear a wool suit
and stand with your arms crossed,
your tie a black wedge mirroring
a starched collar, one white cuff exposed
at your wrist, left hand clenched in a fist.
The photographer lit your face from the left,
leaving the right in half-moon shadow,
your mouth sealed shut in a tight line,
one illuminated eye drilling into mine.
Can you see all my doubts, everything

119

I still don't know? Can you see my beard
turning white, my ambition still burning hot
as the tip of your cigar, the ash breaking apart,
drifting down like the first flakes of November snow?

Richard M. Berlin

How a Psychiatrist Writes a Poem

I begin by remembering
my hours as a patient
and Freud's "Fundamental Rule":

Say Whatever Comes to Mind,
which is the sound of brown leaves
skittering across the sidewalk

on this mild November day
and the smell of smoke
from fires burning in the fields.

Then I relax into my leather chair
and recall the details of this morning-
my wife curled below our down comforter,

her breasts still warm while I dressed,
the texture of walnut bread in my mouth,
the taste of Earl Grey tea.

This is the moment my therapist
would cross his legs, look into my eyes,
and wait for me to reveal something

more painful, closer to my heart,
and just to please him
I might report a few small agonies

from my trip to the session-a delay
for the bridge repair at Rawson Brook,
the red glow from my battery-failure light,

or the threat of anthrax reported on the radio.
I'd say, *Bioterror reminds me of my father's illness.*
And now that I'm talking about my father,

I can see my therapist move forward
in his chair and nod a bit faster
which brings something to mind

I never thought to discuss-
last night's conversation with my mother
who told me she has a melanoma

on her thigh, the thigh I hugged
as a five year old when we shopped
in the aisles of the Grand Union.

I remember those moments
as the closest we ever shared-
the soft, smooth plane of skin,

her delicate gold ankle bracelet,
khaki shorts and Shalimar perfume.
Yes, psychotherapy always leads back

to mother. But before I can resolve
my Oedipal drama in therapy or this poem,
before I can make sense of the grief

I am just beginning to feel.
I hear my therapist say. *Time's up,*
and he stands and gazes outside,

the way I gaze out my office window right now,
noticing how the leaves still cling
to the oak before they let go.

The Discretion of Freud's Reading Chair

*S.F. had the habit of reading in a very peculiar and uncomfortable body position.
He was leaning in this chair, in some sort of diagonal position, one of his legs
slung over the arm of the chair, the book held high and his head unsupported.
The rather bizarre form of the chair I designed is to be explained as an attempt
to maintain this habitual posture and to make it more comfortable.*

—Felix Augenfeld

It was his gift or curse always to seek
the underside, the id that lurks beneath
the ego and super-ego, the naked lust
that drives our noblest deeds. His couch,
draped disarmingly in a Persian rug,
encouraged confession. Reclining
in a parody of ease, patients gave up
their secrets freely in free association.

The censored speech of books he found less
scrutable. He'd choose one from the shelf,
arrange his body like a contortionist
in the chair designed by Augenfeld,
and hold the volume overhead, as though
trying to peek under the skirt of lofty
sentiment or reasoned discourse. It was
his gift or curse, inflicting much dis-ease.

Few pages escaped the penetration
of those gimlet eyes, neatly encircled
by spectacles. Yet their secrets and his
are safe with the chair. That Henry Moore
homunculus has never relaxed or told tales.
It still presides over Freud's study
in London, knowing more than family
or friend about the doctor's underside

Eugene Mahon

First Visit to Bergasse 19

Are these the jackboot
Cobbles Engelmann strode
To take his fated photos?
How ordinary the rooms,
The emptied spaces,
The layout, the encasement
Of books,
Expectation jolted,
As if one
Had returned to womb
In search of home
Only to find
A used lot instead,
Freud,
Known only
Through words and dreams,
Now not known at all.
"But that is ex-
Actly my legacy"
He screams
Through a wooden mouthpiece
"In scraps of dreams

Expect only to find
The blasted ruins of yourself,
Microbes eating plastic
Beneath five fathoms
To set the ocean free."

Richard M. Berlin

Transference

I can't remember what he says
this first session, only his careful attention
and a sense he sees through my camouflage.
I feel I've known him a long time,
familiar as red in the maple outside
or the smell of leather on my father's skin.
When I cry, tissues are at hand,
and when I sob, he listens, alert,
silent, which comforts me and is sufficient.
And I feel closer to him than 50 minutes
should allow, a puzzled sensation
I've known him all my life.
Certain I have chosen wisely,
I reach out to say *Good bye Jerry,*
my dead father's name.

Identification

Freud said Grow a beard
and beards sprang from the cheeks
and chins of analysts
as if they'd put seeds
in their mouths

Freud said Light up your cigars
and the American Psychoanalytic Association
became a tsunami of smoke

Freud said Sit in a chair behind a couch and the army of analysts like
race car drivers at the Grand Prix ran toward their consulting rooms and
assumed their positions

Freud said Say very little to your patients
Make lots of money
Start every paper you write
with some quote from something I've written
no matter how obscure

Freud said If you love me
wear these rings
in memory of me

Lacan said Make it as difficult as you can

Lacan said Use the conditional voice
Write and speak dramatically
hysterically

After all we are the country of Charcot

Lacan said Listen to me fart in public

Lacan said If you love me
you will speak like me
dress like me
fart like me

Anna Freud said Expel Lacan he's a charlatan
and the International Psychoanalytical Association expelled Lacan

Anna Freud said As analysts we are not concerned
with the events in the external world as such
but only with their repercussions in the mind

So much for the Holocaust
which generations of analysts
ignored when dealing with their Jewish analysands

Stolorow said that he invented the word "intersubjectivity"
while drinking a pitcher of beer
with a pal in California

Scores of sycophants
who hadn't read anything but psych books
believed him

Before them all Wilhelm Fleiss told Freud
It's all in the nose

He knows said Freud

A foot and a half of gauze left in Emma Eckstein's nose

Someone in Denmark knows

Arnold Richards

Study Group

Freud asked
what do women want
Not so wise a man
I thought maybe he
didn't know everything.

My students
are women groupies
who hang on every word
and I tell good jokes besides
they think I know everything.

I dazzle
with my erudition
I know them better
than they know themselves.
I bask in their adoration.

They think
I know what women want
and I should tell Freud
But do I know myself or anything?

Fern G.Z. Carr

Freudian Slip

If Sigmund Freud visited
the monkey house
at Vienna's
Tiergarten Schoenbrunn[1]
and happened to
slide on a banana peel,
would that be considered
a Freudian slip?

[1] *Tiergarten Schoenbrunn* is German for Schoenbrunn Zoo

Chris Fogg

The Waitress from Mass Moca[1]

When the waitress from Mass. Moca
turned away to fix my latte
I thought I caught a glimpse of
a slogan on her T-shirt -
Not, you understand, that I'm
in the habit of staring
at girls' chests - but sometimes, you know,
you can't help it, can you? I *mean* -
there are those that shriek at you,
or wink, slyly, like traffic lights:
Walk, Don't Walk. You know the kind?

Get It Here! Hands Off! The Real Thing!
Abandon Hope All Who Dare
To Enter Here - then an arrow
pointing downwards... forbidden fruit -
Big Apple - Big Easy - Big Mac
Make My Day - Do You Feel Lucky?
I'm a Rhinestone Cowboy – An
Urban Guerilla - Eco
Warrior - Kung Fu Fighter
or those that tell you where they've been:

[1] The Massachusetts Museum of Contemporary Art

139

Bowie – The Serious Moonlight
Tour. (*That's* showing my age.
But I often wondered – did *you*? –
how can moonlight be *serious*?)
They seem to promise allegiance –
were you there *too*? Wasn't it *cool*?
Let's put on our red shoes and dance.
I've Been To Idaho And Lived
To Tell The Tale Chicago
White Sox Boston Red Sox The Knicks
The Mets The Yankees The Braves

What do they *mean*? What do they
signify? Belonging? These
badges that we wear like totems?
D'you wanna be in my gang,
My gang, my gang? D'you wanna
Be in..? That's why I fell for
The Leader of the Pack. Yeah, yeah...

Your turn to share the secret...

A picture of my Grandfather
rises before me unbidden -
from the time when Masons were still
acceptable, reputable
even - blindfolded, trusting,
left trouser leg rolled up,
entering the holy temple...

And of course, the ubiquitous
I Love New York - where the word
love is replaced by a red heart.

Like those pictograms we used to
get in the comics. You know?
An eye, followed by a wasp
with the letter 'P' crossed out, then
an 'H', preceding the drawing
of an ear. Have you got it?
I... Was... Here... Go on – work it out.

I Got A Lock Of Britney's Hair
I Threw My Panties At Tom Jones
Bill Clinton Asked Me For a
Blow-Job - who *didn't* he ask? -
But I Turned Him Down. You wanted
to stand out from the crowd? *Hmm...*
Isn't that what we *all* want?

Then there are those that offer guidance:
The Trained Mind Can Conquer Hunger
(Really? Maybe I should try that).
Jesus Loves You May The Force

Be With You. Happiness Is...
What? The T-shirts can't seem
to agree. *Two kinds of ice cream?*
Or *A warm gun?* I never had
any of these... Shit, I did!
I'd quite forgotten. A Native
American stared proudly from
my Anglo-Saxon chest to proclaim...
... *what?* I can't remember now –
something trite about children
being our only hope for
the future. But was it so

trite? I say that *now*, but when
I wore it I guess I bought
into it, wanting to share
it around. In any case I
left it on a beach in Cornwall.

I read somewhere that lots of us
do that, leave clothes behind us, like
animals marking out our
territory, and not just
T-shirts - sweaters, shoes, even
underwear. It's like graffiti
scrawled on walls, school desks, fences:
Kilroy was Here. Jenny loves Max -
True! What Do We Want? Whatever.
When Do We Want It? Now. Now?
Always. Sooner. Yesterday.

"Did you say 'latte', sir, or
'Americano'? Would that be
regular or *decaf*?" Her
T-Shirt turns half toward me -
Proud Of Our Dreams.
Proud of our *dreams*? *Whose* dreams? Does she
Mean *me*? Do we share the same dreams?
I never remember my dreams -
Do *you*? I once had a girlfriend
who, every morning when she woke
up, wrote hers down, then proceeded
to analyze and agonize...

It was boring, but that's not why
we broke up – no, that's a different
story altogether. Though
I do recall her dreams had
nothing at all to do with me...
But the waitress from Mass MoCa –
what does *she* mean? Proud of her dreams.
If we all were proud of our dreams,
we'd put that old fraud Freud
out of a job. And *all* the shrinks...
I've never liked that word, have *you*?
Shrinks. As if they diminish us
somehow. Whereas aren't they meant to
open us out, expand us, like
those flowers you see when time-lapse
photographs run one after the other?
Open, then closed, open, then closed...

And now she turns again, cup in hand,
and walks towards me. "Will there be
anything else?" And I notice
I was wrong. It does not say "dreams".
Not proud of her dreams. But *farms*.
Proud of our Farms. I'm thrown. And she
has to ask me again. "Will that
be all?" No, not all. By no means
all.
        I don't live on a farm.
Do *you*? Does anyone? Any *more*?
Evidently they do, else why
would she invoke us to be proud?
Farmers are in trouble – we *know*,
but then, haven't they *always* been?
What's so special *now*? I *mean* –
who's ever seen a poor farmer?

143

We all of us need to eat, right?
But that's not it, is it? That's not
what she means – at least, that's not
what I *think* she means. For a start
there's no logo, no brand, just words,
black on white, (though not black *and* white).

No glib advertisement phrases –
Eat The View or *East West Home's Best* –
Just words. Bald, plain, unadorned.
As if to say, all of us
have them – farms – stretching away,
acre after acre, endless,
as far as the eye can see. Like
Dreams…
        "That'll be 3 dollars,"
she says. Cheap at half the price
for a mug of latte and dreams!
I sit. "You have a nice day now,"
she chimes, and suddenly I know:
when next I sleep – I'll plough.

Sick Student

"*I look around me, and lo! on every visage a Black Veil!*"
—Mr. Hooper in Hawthorne. "*The Minister's Black Veil*"

Show me your tits
She thinks I say
When I ask *what's all this?*
Tapping her nib-jabbed essay.

The blue ink's run
As if some rage
Had been shotgunned
Upon the page

Before condensing into tears.
She's wearing latex gloves
Because she blurts she fears
An STD from Jesus whom she loves.

Her classroom oddities
Have grown more violent—
Wild flossing, swatting hair-hived bees—
As she bungles each assignment.

I won't record an F,
But ask her to revise.
She hears *fuck me* as if
All words sexualize

Her nails-scraped-blackboard brain.
Her lungs contort each breath;
Talk stokes a raw migraine.
She'd welcome sleep or death,

But has to pass the class.
I broach a therapist –
She lip-reads *want some ass*
And flees across campus.

Infamous among faculty
Who sympathize but fear her
Fixation on obscenity.
She once received honors:

Our grad-school-bound English major.
Her chemistry's a mystery:
The acumen of a scholar
Combined with helpless deviltry.

Such brilliance. And such horror.

Freud

Was it his greatest feat
Perhaps
To make a science of listening,
As if he knew a scream
For what it was,
A storming of deaf ears,
A deafness not of others' making
But our own,
The worst indifference
A self in flight,
Not from the locked out wind,
The banished rain,
But from a wind within,
The heart startled
By its own insistence
Beat after beat after beat?
Did silence,
Like a sobbing child
Bring hidden words to him,
And did he hear them through the tears,
And even find a word for silence,
A word to calm the screaming?

Was it his greatest feat
Perhaps
To call this silence
By its name,
To call it out of its own dreaming,
And lead it home?

What the Computer Doesn't Know

is that numbers don't always add up;
certain words bleed, angry and stinging;
every mountain has the potential
to crush or save us; our orange sun
plagues us with its doggedness;
loneliness is multiple, each of us
harboring seeds of sadness that grow up
to be tornadoes, or broken bricks,
or doors that won't open. Being
human is rain running down streets,
more than the culverts can hold.
Being human is wreckage
in the wake of a smile. Just yesterday,
I held a widower, his hefty frame
hollow despite a certain lovelessness
in the marriage – fifty years
among the armchairs and aisles
and aimlessness filling the grave
more fully than he had imagined.
We can't prepare. The computer
doesn't need to. Today my friend
will eat, drink, surf the internet.
Outside his window: mountain, sun.
Inside: everyone the two of them
ever were. Also no one, a zero sum.

149

Cloak and Dagger

Freud took a knife to the throat
Of the dream
He met on the corner
Of night-town and sleep.
"I am not what I seem"
said the dream.
"Me neither"
Said Freud.
"Forget what I look like"
The dream spluttered at knifepoint.
"To spot the core of me,
Go deeper.
Whatever took place
is no longer on location."

Henry Seiden

From an Analyst's Notebook

Case Report

I thought this would be a hard case:
a shell and only a little softer inside;
a walnut, maybe, the convoluted nut-meat
like two halves of a petrified brain.

I was no stranger to shells:
the egg you're careful not to crack,
the oyster which defies you to crack it,
the lobster you let cook in its own juice.

Then I saw: Oh, I said, an avocado
—leathery, then the soft soap, then
we would get to the impossible pit.

And there would be a ripening
like a mango, like a melon:
the sweetness a kind of dying really,
the way the mother dies
for the sake of the child.

Nancy Scott

Into the Wild

She was in the woods digging
when she came upon
a cache of dreams.

She spread them out
on a pile of dead leaves
carefully detaching
one dream from the other.

A nascent dream quivered
its transparent wings
attempted to fly
but faltered.
Watch me, she said.

She stood on her toes
pressed her face to the wind
swooped and floated
floated and rose
over the treetops
the roofs, the mountains

until she could feel
her bones dissolve
and the dream
slipped alongside her.

Together they soared
shapeless as memory
straying farther and farther
into the wild.

Lori Levy

On Closing the Basement Door

For Connie Day, friend, teacher, mentor

Think of it as a wine cellar, she says,
not a damp dark basement.
Imagine the treasures you might find:
the taste of the grapes …

I keep seeing the door – not how it opens,
but how I rush to close it again and again.
How the chill can seep out
through the tiniest crack.

How sometimes, as though kicked from within,
the door blasts wide open. Cold.
Ghosts. I wrestle with them,
slam the door shut.

How now, with my friend's gentle coaxing,
my hand's on the knob. Almost ready

to try the dark.
Uncork a red.
To test it.

Zara Raab

Fracas in the Street

I saw him on Shattuck,
shouting God knows what –
a man new to madness,
wading half asleep
through his days, weak,
falling over his own life,
consuming himself,
as trees open to hushed
pastures of cheat grass,
and crickets, those leggy,
fragile violinists
of summer verandas,
in times of late rain
hatch all at once in the brush
consuming those before them.
Whole fields they vacuum,
earth heaving them in waves
with rustling of pique
and crackling of crusts.
By the millions they gather
in the desert prairie.

I've known, too, storms of dust
to darken what light remains.
I've known the sudden lunge
to shadows in the road
when too long I waited,
fevered to be fed.

Susan Wheatley

The Winter Meetings of the Freudians

The winter meetings of the Freudians
used to be held—maybe still are—
at the Waldorf Astoria Hotel,

the name of which she knew when she was young
(as much as one can know anything)
only as a six-layer cake, her favorite,

which her mother made for birthdays in Ohio:
the Waldorf Astoria Red Velvet Cake,
with its now-banned quarter-cup of red dye #4.

Back then, on her eighteenth birthday,
returning to college from break,
she made the mistakes

of flying into Newark, not LaGuardia,
and of taking a bus not to Grand Central
but to the Newark train station

late at night to catch the Amtrak.
She found the platform and waited
with three other souls, two in baseball jackets,

one sleeping in rags,
until, after two hours, a disembodied voice
announced that Amtrak was delayed to 4 AM.

And the two men in jackets approached her,
as she pretended to fall asleep
over her homework on the Aeneid,

but they were friendly and said
she wouldn't be safe here,
to come with them for coffee

and so she did, and she sat
between them in their pickup truck.
Then at the diner, in a booth

with steamed-up windows, they told her
about their home in Jersey City and how
they didn't like Newark, or New York either.

Then they returned her to the platform
having perhaps saved her from a mugging
or at least a long night in the echoing station

they did not know, any of them,
that later she would tell this story
because of a cake

named for the hotel
where the Freudians hold their winter meetings,
the tribe that might dare to claim

that the red dye, the mother, the birthday,
the strangers at the train station,
were all in her mind connected.
But I tell you now
that if there is one thing I know
it is that sometimes a cake,

however red, dangerous,
or forced into associations it might be,
is still nothing more than a cake.

The Best Thing for It

Trouble catching your breath? Some
kind of serpent's put the squeeze on
your ribs. Or it's one
tentacle of the inevitable
in a thoughtless coil around

your heart's crushable crib. You're gasping
a little. You're blinking
and so is the room around you, now
that your aorta doesn't seem to be sluicing
much blood to that pair of carotids, does it?

Maybe it's just your time
and someone in an ER will call it
cardiac. Or severe allergic
bronchospastic reaction to what
must be the dust of hazelnuts, just

a touch, just because
the chef ran out of nutmeg to sharpen
the crème anglaise. Or have you been
shot in the back by a maniac, right
through the windpipe, and breathlessness

trumps what would be a searing pain
up your spine? That's a fine way
to make sense of the sudden
air hunger. Though maybe it's panic
alone paralyzing your diaphragm, not

a thing in the world. Remember
how you were laid down for another
and then another forever before
you were two? No, you don't, but
your mother just meant to light a next smoke.

Who knew it scared you stiff, your chest
gripping its own existence? This is
what's got you now, and the best
thing for it you know is the oceany
breath of your fresh-lit cigarette.

R. Bremner

In Paterson, at Blimpie's

In Paterson, at Blimpie's
sit Aristotle and Descartes
at a plastic table
in plastic chairs
watching through the blue plate glass
for their bus to Fair Lawn
while outside in the slush mess
stands a huddle of shiverers
waiting too.
And "Aw, shuddup!" says Aristotle.
"NO, you shuddup!" says Descartes.
They giggle frantically in
appreciation of each other's wit.
Meanwhile at the back table
sits Sigmund Freud carefully
tempering his coffee with cream,
studying intensely the play
being acted out before him
while Holden Caulfield sweeps the floor.
And "Aw, shuddup!" says Aristotle.
"NO, you shuddup!" says Descartes.
After many shuddups
the Fair Lawn bus arrives.

Aristotle and Descartes
guffaw frantically, fraternally
as they charge through Blimpie's door
while Sigmund, unsmiling still,
sips his weak brew
and outside the cream pours onto the bus
an inside Holden sweeps Blimpie's floor.

(This concerns an actual incident in 1979, when I was a student at ECPI on Market Street in Paterson, New Jersey. One winter's day I was sitting in the "Blimpie Base" at Main and Market, wasting time before my Main Line train back to Passaic, when the incident unfolded.)

Freudians, Keep Out

A bee's *beeness* is never discrete—but the hive is. *We* is
another. Even in travel, nobody dances because nobody
exists.

Within the hive *communicants* feel one meaning as they
move—in concentric rings in winter, other times moving
across.

Outside—*beeness* has no meaning other than "C'mon!"—
felt, of course, although nobody exists.

Honey makes itself. It, too, is another.

And you?

Summary

Deprivation precedes greed.
Rage follows humiliation.
Vanity masks hollowness.
Glamour seeks solace.
Lust blinds reason.
Logic mutes passion.
Envy spoils admiration.
Pity harbors disgust.
Ambition corrupts talent.
Surprise implies innocence.
Learning acknowledges ignorance.
Guilt accompanies gratitude.
Humility respects history.
Love sustains all.

Freud Quiz

FREUD QUIZ #1

Freud in German means

(a) Fright

(b) Joy

(c) Sauteed lightly in olive oil

(d) "The young eagle, a rank impostor, fled the Reich."

(e) The same thing "it" means in German.[1]

FREUD QUIZ # 2

According to Freud in *The Future of an Illusion*, what is an illusion?

(a) A falsehood

(b) Something that may be true or may come true but probably won't.

(c) Religion.

(d) Art

(e) A ghost in the sense intended by Ibsen in his play *Ghosts.*

---

[1] I would guess (e) because of the quote marks. My reasoning: It is obvious that Freud is greater than the sum of his disciples (d), and I would argue that (a) is archaic, and (b) is accurate only if one approves of Beethoven's translation of Schiller. So that leaves (c) and (e) and the former is too York 40s rather than New York today. The real question is whether 'it' is (1) the id, (2) Freud as a proper noun, i.e. a signifier with surplus meaning, or (3) the universal pronoun." —John Casebeer

FREUD QUIZ # 3

What does "beyond the pleasure principle" refer to?

(a) A book by Sigmund Freud.

(b) A vast right-wing conspiracy.

(c) Death.

(d) The dark side of the moon considered as an image for female sexuality.

(e) The sadness following orgasm.

(f) The unconscious.

(g) The desire to retreat into the womb.

(h) The heroine's disastrous first marriage.

FREUD QUIZ # 4

Freud came up with great titles, which poets like to steal, and the best of these is

(a) *The Interpretation of Dreams*

(b) *Jokes and Their Relation to the Unconscious*

(c) *Civilization and Its Discontents*

(d) *The Problem of Anxiety*

(e) *Totem and Taboo*

FREUD QUIZ # 5

What is the "compulsion to repeat"?

(a) the impulse to keep doing the thing that scares you—in an effort to master the fear

(b) the reason why Hitler copied Napoleon's disastrous invasion of Russia

(c) the need to repeat the same futile action and the madness of expecting a different result

(d) the rhetorical strategy of using the same word (or an anagram of it) in every sentence of a paragraph

(e) the belief that history doesn't repeat itself but it sometimes rhymes

(f) voting for candidates named Kennedy, Clinton, or Bush

FREUD QUIZ # 6

Psychoanalysis became known as the "talking cure" because

(a) it depends on free association

(b) all talk and no action make Jack a dull boy

(c) it was the talk of Viennese café society

(d) he heard a woman's voice in a dream: "she'll be riding six white horses when she comes." And he woke up feeling pretty good.[2]

(e) the shrink with the hearing aid is the single greatest metaphor for the profession since Groucho Marx told a mother of eight that he liked his cigar a lot but took it out of his mouth once in a while, and the conversation went on from there.

FREUD QUIZ # 7

In Freud's view, when the Dalai Lama met Salvador Dali

(a) they discussed a possible merger of Surrealism and Buddhism.

(b) they criticized US foreign policy.

(c) they were in a Gap commercial for khaki trousers.

(d) they sang "Hello, Dolly."

(e) it was like the meeting of an umbrella and a sewing machine on an operating table.

FREUD QUIZ # 8[3]

If Jacques Lacan had written "Beyond the Pleasure Principle," death would be

(a) A one-way ticket to Palookaville

(b) The big sleep

(c) A modern office building

(d) A seventeenth-century orgasm

(e) The mirror

[2] Compare the last line of Philip Roth's *Portnoy's Complaint* with that of Norman Mailer's *The Naked and the Dead*.

[3] "Freud Quiz" is supported by a grant from the tomb.

FREUD QUIZ # 9

(a) Who wrote the *Confessions* of Rousseau?

(b) Who wrote the *Confessions of Nat Turner?*

(c) Who wrote the *Confessions of a Justified Sinner?*

(d) Who wrote the *Autobiography of Alice B. Toklas?*

(e) Who played Boswell to Samuel Johnson?

FREUD QUIZ # 10

Freud, an avowed agnostic, said that he remained culturally Jewish. The best evidence for this is

(a) the skullcap that he wore when having sex with his wife

(b) in no photograph do you ever see Freud smile

(c) Freud compiled a joke book as diligently as he collected dreams and errors

(d) he refused to take a Rorschach Test

(e) he left Vienna for London rather than die at the hands of the Nazis

FREUD QUIZ # 11

Freud maintained that death was

(a) the best of a bad business

(b) the best of both worlds

(c) the maiden

(d) one of the two unknowns in the equation

(e) the greater of two evils

BONUS POINTS:

Auden concludes his elegy for Freud by saying, "Sad is Eros, builder of cities, / And weeping anarchic Aphrodite." What makes Auden call Eros – the impish god of love, known in Latin as Cupid—"builder of cities"?

FREUD QUIZ # 12

At which of these jokes did Freud laugh:

(a) Catholic is to wholesale as Protestant is to retail

(b) "A wife is like an umbrella. Sooner or later you take a cab."

(c) "This girl is like Dreyfus. The army doesn't believe in her innocence."

(d) "Was your mother once in service at the palace?" "No, your Highness, but my father was."

(e) Blind man: "Wie gehts." Lame man: "As you see."

FREUD QUIZ # 13

What do women want?

(a) what they have

(b) what they don't have

(c) a cigar

(d) R-E-S-P-E-C-T

(e) next question

FREUD QUIZ # 14

Freud's discovery of "drives" came about because

(a) some dreams cannot be ascribed to wish-fulfillment.

(b) when Freud played golf in Scotland, he favored drivers over putters

(c) he was inspired by Walter Donaldson song "You're Driving Me Crazy"

(d) there were more things in heaven and hell than are dreamed of in your philosophy

(e) there was no other way to explain death.

FREUD QUIZ # 15

When John Huston made a movie of Freud's life, whom did he cast in the part of the Viennese father of psychoanalysis?

(a) John Huston's own father Walter.

(b) Montgomery Ward

(c) Montgomery Clift

(d) George Montgomery

(e) Huston never made a movie of Freud's life

(f) Anthony Perkins in fright wig.

(g) Susanna York

FREUD QUIZ # 16

In addition to John Huston's *Freud*, which of these movies deal with the papa of psychoanalysis:

(f) Orson Welles's "The Trial" in which Joseph K. (Anthony Perkins)—and by extension Kafka himself—is understood to be Freud's anti-type and thus, by Freudian logic, Freud himself.

(g) Orson Welles's "Chimes at Midnight" in which Freud (Orson Welles) cavorts after hours with tippling cronies and good-natured prostitutes.

(h) Kurosawa's "Throne of Blood" in which Freud is depicted as a version of Macbeth, with Mrs. Freud (Lady MacBeth) providing the brains and the drive of the operation.

(i) Hitchcock's "Spellbound" in which Gregory Peck is an amnesiac, Ingrid Bergman is his analyst, and Freud is Ingrid Bergman's father in upstate New York

(j) Sam Peckinpah's "The Wild Bunch," an allegory about the triumph of Freud's ego psychology (William Holden) over rival theories of the universe such as those of Karl Marx (the Mexicans), Lenin (the machine gun), and Jacques Derrida (the scorpions). Ernest Borgnine plays Freud's wife and Robert Ryan is Jung. Also starring Ben Johnson as Ben Jonson and Warren Oates as himself. Holden (giving an order): "Let's go." Oates: "Why not?" For extra credit, what is the last thing Holden says in the movie?

FREUD QUIZ # 17

In what movie does a murder suspect tell a bearded, benevolent psycho-analysis, "Freud is hooey"?

CLUES:

(a) "Women make the best analysts until they get married. Then they make the best patients."

(b) The seven of clubs.

(c) She is glad he didn't dream of her as an egg beater, as another of her patients had done.

(d) "Any husband of Constance is a husband of mine."

(e) The proprietor had a small wheel in his hand.

(f) The hero registered as John Brown in the hotel.

FREUD QUIZ # 18

The reason you never see Freud smiling in a photograph is
(a) he kept a straight face at all times
(b) he refused to smile on command
(c) Viennese professors took pride in their solemnity
(d) psychoanalysis was a joke, but he didn't want to give the game away
(e) photography was still in its infancy

FREUD QUIZ # 19

The stated agenda of *Moses and Monotheism* is
(a) Moses was an Egyptian
(b) Monotheism was an advance on polytheism because the concentration of divinity in a single
(c) entity meant that man could solve for equations with two unknowns in elementary algebra
(d) Moses went to the wilderness in a vain effort to account for his fatherlessness
(e) Peace in the Middle East
(f) If you tell an animal joke, your chances of getting a laugh will improve if you make the animal
(g) a duck.

FREUD QUIZ # 20

To explain how man acquired the power of fire, Freud appeals to which of the following:
(a) The story of Prometheus, the Titan, who stole the fire of the gods and gave it to humankind, hidden in a phallic-shaped hollow rod. For this crime he was punished most vilely: each day a vulture feasted on his liver, which in ancient times was regarded as the seat of all passion and desires.
(b) The organ that Heine describes in these lines: "Was dem Menscen dient zum Seichen / Damit schafft er Seinesgleichen." [With that which serves a man to piss / He reproduces is own kind.] The child thinks he can do both things at once. But the adult knows that "the two acts are as incompatible as fire and water."

(c) The fact that the penis is sometimes in a fiery state of excitation that justifies calling it a cock in English (or a vogel, or bird in German). In such a state, urination is impossible

(d) The example of fictional characters such as Gargantua and Pantagruel in Rabelais and Gulliver in Swift, who put out fires by pissing on them, dramatizing that such an action is natural and instinctive and must be renounced by mankind if we are going to achieve civilization and its attendant discontents.

(e) Hercules can achieve his triumph over the hydra-headed water-snake of Lerna only when he uses fire to burn out the snake's one immortal head—which seems counter to the thrust of our argument until we "reverse the manifest content."

FREUD QUIZ # 21

A Freudian slip is

(a) A courteous form letter from *New Yorker* declining to print your latest effort "despite its obvious merit."

(b) A patch of a woman's white slip strategically exposed beneath her skirt or dress.

(c) The inability to keep a secret, usually but not always sexual.

(d) The laughter aroused when a rotund man slips on a banana peel and flies spectacularly to a hard landing on the pavement.

(e) A mistake attributable to deep subconscious elements in the human psyche.

(f) An error, as in the joke Jung told Freud about the man, the woman, and the duck entering a bar, which resulted in Jung's expulsion from the movement on the grounds that either *woman* or *duck* was code for *Jew* in that joke.[4]

(g) A pyrrhic victory, or déjà-vu in French.

---

[4] A pig figures in the joke but in a purely rhetorical sense.

FREUD QUIZ # 22

One August day in 1909 Freud fainted in Jung's company because

(a) He was eating lunch and the schnitzel disagreed with him.

(b) He felt a sexual attraction to Jung.

(c) Freud had slept with his wife's younger sister and Jung threatened to blackmail him after hearing him talk about it in his sleep on the trip the two men took to America.

(d) They were having an argument about something trivial when Jung revealed himself to be a virulent anti-Semite. "You're next," he said with an evil laugh. He kept repeating, Jude Jude Jude.

(e) Either Freud said the father of monotheism must have hated his own father and Jung gave him a dirty look, or Jung told Freud the joke about the man, the woman, and the duck entering a bar.

(f) Jung said the spring weather made him feel like a young man. From this innocuous remark, Freud knew that Jung was an impostor. "You were never Jung!" Freud cried.

FREUD QUIZ # 23

Where did Freud and Dante hold their first summit meeting?

(a) The Sands Hotel in Las Vegas, 1962

(b) The Minetta Tavern in Greenwich Village

(c) With Ulysses and Diomedes in the Eighth Circle of *The Inferno*

(d) Stanza 14 of Auden's elegy for Freud.

(e) Omaha Beach on June 6, 1944

(f) AA

(g) In New York City's war on crime

FREUD QUIZ # 24

Where and when did Freud die, and of what cause?

(a) At Freiberg (then part of Moravia) of a gunshot wound said to be self-inflicted on 6 May 1856

(b) In London of throat cancer on 23 September 1939

(c) Brokenhearted in North London of so-called natural causes on March 14, 1883

(d) In Paris, executed by guillotine, 28 July 1794

(e) In the saddle on January 26, 1979

(f) Of food poisoning a week after the publication of *Traumdeutung* in Vienna on November 1899

FREUD QUIZ # 25:

What were Freud's last words?

(a) *Mehr licht! Mehr licht!*

(b) More beer!

(c) Either the wallpaper goes, or I do.

(d) Friends, applaud! The comedy is finished.

(e) Don't let it end like this. Tell them I said something.

(f) Am I dying or is it my birthday?

Afterword

PART OF OUR INTENTION, as indicated in the grant proposal, was to follow the publication of the anthology with educational outreach in a variety of ways.

After launching the book with a poetry reading by some of the contributors, we hope to follow with other readings in various appropriate locations. By this we mean, not just bookstores and libraries, but also colleges, universities, creative writing programs and centers for training psychologists, psychiatrists, social workers and other mental health professionals.

Just as we have assembled an eclectic group of poets in this volume, we anticipate that our readers will also be an eclectic group. Many will be professional poets and teachers of literature and creative writing to undergraduate and graduate students. Some will be leaders of poetry workshops and book discussion groups who have only a layperson's knowledge (which may be considerable, considering the "climate of opinion") of psychoanalysis and Freudian theory. Others will be mental health professionals who would like to know more about poetry.

Students and participants in all of these groups, as well as the leaders themselves, may want to do some background reading. For that purpose, the list below, a mixture of new and old but not outdated titles, may be helpful.

Suggestions for Supplementary Reading

Bach, Sheldon (2016) *Chimera and Other Writings*. New York: International Psychoanalytic Books.

Brenner, Charles (1974) *An Elementary Textbook of Psychoanalysis, Revised Edition*. New York: Anchor Press/Doubleday.

Crews, Frederick (2017) "Freud: What's Left?" *New York Review of Books* Vol. LXIV, Number 3.

Felman, Shoshana, Editor (1982) *Literature and Psychoanalysis, The Question of Reading: Otherwise*. Baltimore: The Johns Hopkins University Press.

Gass, William (1976) *On Being Blue: A Philosophical Inquiry*. Boston: David R. Godine.

Heidegger, Martin (1971) *Poetry, Language, Thought, Translated by Albert Hofstadter*. New York: Harper & Row.

Holland, Norman N. (1998) " Freud and the Poet's Eye: His Ambivalence Toward the Artist. " *PsyArt: An Online Journal for the Psychological Study of the Arts* 3/30/2016.

Jacobson, Sheri (2013) " Sigmund Freud's Main Theories in Psychoanalysis: A Summary." Retrieved from www.harleytherapy.co.uk /counselling

Mandel, Charlotte (2004) "The Psychoanalytic Hour As Received Form." *Fulcrum: an annual of poetry and aesthetics,* No. 3, 2004.

Miller, J. David (2016) " The Shared Creative Realm of Psychoanalysis and the Arts." *The American Psychoanalyst,* Vol. 50, No. 3

Phillips, Adam (2001) *Promises, Promises: Essays on Psychoanalysis and Literature*. New York: Basic Books.

Richards, Arlene Kramer (2016) " Poetry and Psychoanalysis: Two Measures of Passion." Unpublished paper. Used by permission of the author.

Richards, Arnold (2015) *Psychoanalysis: Critical Conversations, Selected Papers by Arnold D. Richards, Vol. 1, Edited by Arthur A. Lynch.* New York: Contemporary Freudian Society(CSF) and International Psychoanalytic Books(IP Books).

Roudinesco, Elisabeth (2016) *Freud in His Time and Ours* Translated by Catherine Porter. Cambridge, MA: Harvard University Press.

Rukeyser, Muriel (1996) *The Life of Poetry, With a New Foreword by Jane Cooper.* Ashfield, Massachusetts: Paris Press.

Ruitenbeek, Hendrik M., Editor (1964) *Psychoanalysis and Literature.* New York: E.P. Dutton & Co., Inc.

Seiden, Henry M. (2004). On Relying on Metaphor: What Psychoanalysts Might Learn from Wallace Stevens. *Psychoanalytic Psychology,* Vol. 21, No. 3.

Von Unwerth, Matthew (2005). *Freud's Requiem: Mourning, Memory, and the Invisible History of a Summer Walk.* New York: Riverhead Books.

Wheelock, John Hall (1963) *What Is Poetry?* New York: Charles Scribner's Sons.

Willis, Irene (2007 "A Working Poet Comments on Caston's 'Poetic Closure, Psychoanalytic Termination and Death." *Journal of the American Psychoanalytic Association.*

Notes on Contributors

SALMAN AKHTAR is Professor of Psychiatry at Jefferson Medical College, Philadelphia, PA. and a Supervising and Training Analyst at the Psycho-analytic Center of Philadelphia. A prolific contributor to the psychoanalytic literature, he is also the author of seven collections of poems, three in English and four in his native Urdu, and editor of *Between Hours: A Collection of Poems by Psychoanalysts*.

W.H. AUDEN needs little introduction. An English poet born in 1907, he later became an American citizen. His poems are among the best-known in the English language. He died in 1973.

MILTON J. BATES is the author of a number of non-fiction books. His poems have appeared in many anthologies and magazines, such as the *Bellevue Literary Review* and *The Southern Review*. Five Oaks Press published his chapbook, *Always on Fire* in 2016, nominating one of the poems for a Pushcart Prize.

RICHARD M. BERLIN is the author of three books of poems: *How JFK Killed My Father, Secret Wounds,* and *Practice*. His poetry has appeared monthly in *Psychiatric Times* for the past seventeen years, and his most recent work was published in *Liberation: New Works by Internationally Renowned Poets*. He is the winner of numerous awards, including the Pearl Poetry Prize, the John Ciardi Prize in Poetry, and the USA Book News Award, which chose *Secret Wounds* as the best poetry book published in America in 2011. A Senior Affiliate in Psychiatry at the University of Massachusetts Medical School, he practices psychiatry in the Berkshire hills of western Massachusetts.

187

EMILY BERRY lives in London, England. Her debut collection of poems, *Dear Boy* (Faber & Faber, 2013) won the Hawthornden Prize and the Forward Prize for Best First Collection. She received an Eric Gregory Award in 2008. Her second collection, *Stranger, Baby*, is forthcoming from Faber& Faber in 2017. It was announced recently that she has just succeeded Maurice Riordan as the new Editor of *The Poetry Review*, one of the most widely read poetry magazines in the U. K.

MAROULA BLADES is an Afro-British poet and writer living in Berlin. The winner of the Caribbean Writer 2014 Flash Fiction Competition and Erbacce Prize in 2012, her first poetry collection, *Blood Orange*, was published by Erbacce-press. Her work has also appeared in many anthologies and magazines, and a poetry/music program by her has been presented on several stages in Germany. Her debut EP-album, *Word Pulse*, is released by Havavision Records (UK)

LAUREL BLOSSOM, an award-winning poet and editor, is the author of two book-length, narrative prose poems, *Degrees of Latitude* and *Longevity*, both from Four-Way books. Her previous books of lyric poetry include *Wednesday: New and Selected Poems, The Papers Said, What's Wrong*, and a chapbook, *Any Minute*. She is the editor of *Splash: Great Writing About Swimming*, and is the first-ever Poet Laureate of Edgefield, South Carolina.

R. BREMNER has worked as a cab driver, a truck unloader, a computer programmer, and a vice-president at a major bank. He is widely published, in such places as *International Poetry Review*, as well as in many other magazines, ten e-books and two print books. He received Honorable Mention for the Allen Ginsberg Award in 2016.

CHARLES W. BRICE is a former psychoanalyst and faculty member of the Pittsburgh Psychoanalytic Institute. His full-length poetry collection, *Flashcuts Out of Chaos,* was published in 2016 by WordTech Editions, and his poetry has appeared or is forthcoming in over 45 journals and anthologies.

FERN G.Z. CARR, who lives in British Columbia, is president of Project Literacy, a lawyer, teacher and past President of the Society for the Prevention of Cruelty to Animals. A full member and former Poet-in-Residence for the League of Canadian Poets, this Pushcart Prize nominee also composes and translates poetry in six languages, including Mandarin. Her own poems have been published extensively, from Finland to Mauritius. She has been cited as a contributor to the Prakalpana Literary Movement in India and has had her work recognized by the Parliamentary Poet Laureate. One of her poems is currently orbiting the planet Mars aboard NASA's Maven spacecraft.

ANNE CARSON is a well-known Canadian poet and professor of classics who incorporates themes from many fields in her writing. She frequently refers to and translates Greek literature. She has published twenty books, most of which blend different genres – poetry, essay, prose, criticism, translation, dramatic dialogue, fiction and non-fiction. She has won so many awards for her work that there is scarcely room to list them all. Among them have been a Guggenheim, a Lannan Literary Award, a T.S. Eliot Prize and a MacArthur Fellowship.

WILLIAM ORAL ROBERT COOMBES, named after the 1950's U.S. Traveling Evangelist, Oral Roberts, was born in Oshawa, Ontario, in 1952 and adopted shortly thereafter by an older couple. He tells us that, after being removed from his family of origin, he grew up attending the same schools and living in the same neighborhood as genetic siblings, to which he attributes "an extended identity crisis" and many more problems. He believes that writing about his life and producing abstract/expressionist art have helped him "to recognize some of the gifts received from life experiences." He now lives in a small town in Saskatchewan, Canada, and is a member of the Saskatchewan Writers' Guild.

JAMES CUMMINS is the author of five poetry collections, the most recent of which, *Still Some Cake,* was published by Carnegie Mellon University Press in 2012. One of his books, *Jim and Dave Defeat the Masked Man,*

(Soft Skull Press), was co-authored with David Lehman, whose work is also included in this anthology. He has been published in many journals such as *Paris Review, The Yale Review, The American Poetry Review, Harper's* and *Partisan Review* and has had poems selected for five *Best American Poetry* volumes and a number of other anthologies, including *The Oxford Book of American Poetry* and *180 More.* His poems have been featured on *Poetry Daily, Verse Daily, The Writer's Almanac* and elsewhere, including, in April 2017, *Poetry Monday* in *International Psychoanalysis.* He works as the curator of the Elliston Poetry Collection at the University of Cincinnati, where he is a Professor of English.

TOM DALEY, a recipient of the Dana Award in Poetry, has had poems in *Harvard Review, Massachusetts Review, Fence, Denver Quarterly, Crazyhorse, Witness* and elsewhere. Future/Cycle Press published his first full-length collection of poems, *House You Cannot Reach—Poems in the Voice of My Mother and Other Poems,* in 2015.

TOI DERRICOTTE is a widely-published poet who has won special recognition for her four collections: *The Undertaker's Daughter* (University of Pittsburgh Press, 2011); *Tender* (University of Pittsburgh Press, 1997), winner of the 1998 Paterson Poetry Prize; *Natural Birth* (Crossing Press,1983), and *The Empress of the Death House* (Lotus Press, 1978), as well as for her memoir, *The Black Notebooks,* which won the 1998 Annisfield-Wolf Book Award for non-fiction. She is also well-known as the co-founder, with poet Cornelius Eady, of the Cave Canem Foundation, a national organization committed to cultivating the artistic and professional growth of African-American poets. In 2016, for their work at Cave Canem, she and Eady were awarded the National Book Foundation's Literarian Award for Outstanding Service to the American Literary Community.

STEPHEN DOBYNS has published more than twelve collections of poetry, the most recent of which is *The Day's Last Light Reddens the Leaves of the Copper Beech*(2016). He has been a reporter for the *Detroit News* and has taught at many colleges and universities, including Sarah Lawrence,

Warren Wilson College, the University of Iowa, Syracuse University and Boston University. He is also a fiction writer, whose work includes a collection of short-stories, *Eating Naked;* a novel, *The Wrestler's Cruel Study*, and several mysteries and thrillers, one of which, *The Church of Dead Girls*, has been optioned by HBO. Many readers are familiar with his collection of essays on poetry, *Best Words, Best Order*. His poems have been anthologized in *Best American Poems*, and two of his short-stories selected for *Best American Stories*.

HILDA DOOLITTLE, who used the pen name, H.D., was an early patient of Freud's. It's understood that she consulted him on the issue of her bi-sexuality. Her conflicted attitude toward him is apparent in her famous poem, "The Master." What Freud did for her (and for us) was to encourage her poetry, which was also supported by Ezra Pound. Before she became famous, H.D. studied at Bryn Mawr College for two years, but she dropped out and went to live and write in New York and England.

JUDITHA DOWD'S poetry and prose have appeared in a variety of publications, including *Spillway, The Florida Review, Kestrel,* and *Ekphrasis;* new poems are forthcoming in *Poet Lore* and *Canary*. Her full-length collection, *Mango in Winter*, was published in 2013. She is a member of the U.S. I Poets Cooperative in Princeton, New Jersey and the performance ensemble, "Cool Women."

MERRIDAWN DUCKLER is a poet and playwright from Portland, Oregon. Her poem, "Advice for the Birds," was nominated for 2016 Best of the Web. She was manuscript finalist at Center for Book Arts and Tupelo Press, as well as finalist for the 2016 Sozoplo Fiction Fellowship and the Oregon Play Prize. Awarded numerous fellowships and awards for her writing in all genres, she is an editor of *Narrative* and the international philosophy journal, *Eventual Aesthetics.*

LISKEN VAN PELT DUS was raised in England, the U.S. and Mexico, and now lives in Massachusetts, where she teaches high school and martial arts. Her poetry can be found in literary journals such as *Conduit, The*

South Carolina Review, Cider Press Review and many others, as well as in her chapbook, *Everywhere at Once* and a full-length collection, *What We're Made Of* (Cherry Grove Collections, 2016).

LYNN EMANUEL, who was born in Mt. Kisco, New York, is the author of five collections of poetry, the newest of which is *The Nerve of It: Poems New and Selected* (University of Pittsburgh Press, 2015), which was awarded the 2016 Lenore Marshall Poetry Prize. Another of her books, *Then, Suddenly,* received the Eric Matthieu King Award from the Academy of American Poets. An earlier volume, *The Dig,* was selected by Gerald Stern for the National Poetry Series. Other honors include two fellowships from the National Endowment for the Arts and a fellowship from the Civitella Ranieri Foundation. She has taught at a number of colleges, including Bennington, Warren Wilson, and Vermont, and is currently a professor of English and Creative Writing at the University of Pittsburgh.

CHRIS FOGG, who lives in Dorset, England, is the author of two recent collections of poems and short stories, both published by Mudlark Press. He is also a producer, director and dramaturg who has directed plays for New Perspectives, Farnham Maltings and Strike a Light, as well as productions of his own work, including, in 2016, *Posting to Iraq* for the inaugural Women & War Festival in London, *All the Ghosts Walk with Us* for Bristol Old Vic and *Tree House,* which toured across the south of England. As a dramaturg he has worked with Shobana Jeyasing (South Bank), Alexander Whitley (Sadler's Wells, Royal Opera House, Winter Light Festival New York) Lost Dog (2011 winner of The Place Prize) and Mark Bruce (Sky Arts Award winner 2014). He is currently Creative Producer for the Bonnie Bird Choreography Fund, supporting the work of Ben Duke, Rosemary Lee and Nicola Canibere.

ANNA FREUD was a daughter of Sigmund Freud and was also one of his patients. In the mid-1920's, when she was 30, she acquired a dog named Wolf, a German Shepherd that her father fell in love with. The story is that she became jealous of the dog's place in his life and, as a joke, for one of his birthdays she gave him a picture of Wolf, which he hung in his office. For each of her father's birthdays after Wolf came into their lives, Anna also wrote a poem about the dog, which she would attach to the animal's collar before sending him in to see her father. The picture of the dog was still hanging in his office in Bergasse 19 in 1938, when he was forced to leave Vienna.

CYNTHIA READ GARDNER'S poems have been published in *Alaska Quarterly Review, Southern Poetry Review, The Bridge,* and various anthologies, such as *Crossing Paths: An Anthology of Poems by Women* (Mad River Press, 2007). A chapbook, *How Will They Find Me,* was published by Finishing Line Press in 2012. She has been employed as a clinical social worker for many years and lives in Pittsfield, Massachusetts.

DEBORAH GERRISH is an award-winning poet whose poems appear in many literary magazines. She is the author of *The Language of Paisley and the Language of Rain,* holds an MFA in Poetry from Drew University, and received an Edward Fry Fellowship from Rutgers University. She serves on the Board of Trustees for Women Who Write, Inc., and teaches poetry writing at Fairleigh Dickinson University. Her latest collection of poems, *Light in Light,* is forthcoming.

DAVID GIANNINI'S collections of poetry include *Faces Somewhere Wild* (Dos Madres Press), *Rickshaw Chasm* (Feral Press), *Four Plus Four* (Country Valley Press) and *Span of Thread* (Cervena Barva Press). His limited edition collection called *The Future Only Rattles When You Pick It Up,* which came out in 2016, can be ordered directly from its publisher, Feral Press (Prehensile Pencil Press). *Porous Borders,* a collection of prose poems, has just been published by Spuyten Duyvil. He curates a popular poetry reading series in Berkshire County, Massachusetts.

LOUISE GLÜCK, born in New York City, grew up on Long Island, NY, and lives in Cambridge, Massachusetts. She was Poet Laureate of the United States in 2003, is a Chancellor of the Academy of American Poets, and currently Writer-in-Residence at Yale University. The latest of her twelve books is *Faithful and Virtuous Night* (Farrar, Straus & Girous, 2014). Among her many awards are the Pulitzer Prize, the National Book Critics Circle Award, the Bollingen Prize for Poetry, and the Wallace Stevens Award from the Academy of American Poets.

DIANA GOETSCH'S poetry collection, *The Job of Being Everybody* won the 2003 Cleveland State University Poetry Center Open Competition. Her other books are *Nobody's Hell* (Hanging Loose Press, 1999) and three award-winning chapbooks. Her work also appears in *Poetry 180: A Poem a Day for American High Schools* (Random House, 2003). Many other honors for her work include two Pushcart Prize nominations. A resident of New York City, she teaches in public schools and at Passages Academy in the Bronx, where she teaches creative writing to incarcerated teens.

JEAN HOLLANDER has published five individual volumes of poetry, as well as a 296-page collection, *And They Shall Wear Purple: New and Selected Poems* (Sheep Meadow Press, 2016), distributed by The University Press of New England. Hundreds of her poems have appeared in literary journals, as well as in Best Poem anthologies. Her verse translation of Dante's *Divine Comedy* (with her husband, Dante scholar Robert Hollander) was published by Doubleday and widely acclaimed. The city of Florence awarded her a medal for her work.

VASILIKI KATSAROU lives in western New Jersey, where she is a Geraldine R. Dodge teaching poet who read her work at the 2014 Dodge Poetry Festival. She holds a B.A. magna cum laude from Harvard College and an MFA in film from Boston University. Her first collection, *Memento Tsunami,* was published in 2011, and one of its poems was nominated for a Pushcart Prize. Poems of hers have appeared in many well-known literary magazines in the U.S., UK and Australia and in a number of anthologies, including *Rabbit Ears (TV Poems), Somewhere Else But Here: A Contemporary Anthology of Women and Place.* She has also co-edited two anthologies: *Eating Her Wedding Dress: A Collection of Clothing Poems* and *Dark as a Hazel Eye: Coffee & Chocolate Poems.*

PHILIP LARKIN is another who needs little introduction to those familiar with English literature. Born in 1922, he worked for most of his life as a librarian and became one of England's most eminent poets, considered one of the greatest of the latter half of the twentieth century. He died in 1985.

JOSH LEFKOWITZ won the 2012 Wergle Flomp Humor Poetry Prize, an Avery Hopwood Award for Poetry at the University of Michigan, was a finalist for the 2014 Brooklyn Non-Fiction Prize, and won First Prize in the 2016 Singapore Poetry Contest. His poems and essays have been published in *Barrelhouse, Conduit* and many other places. He has also recorded humor pieces for NPR's "All Things Considered" and BBC's "Americana." He was a poet in residence at the Berkeley Repertory Theatre in summer 2016.

DAVID LEHMAN'S name is familiar to readers, not only as a poet but also as Editor of *The Oxford Book of American Poetry* and Series Editor of *The Best American Poetry,* which he initiated in 1988. He is also Poetry Chair of the New School Writing Program and General Editor of the University of Michigan Press's *Poets on Poetry* Series. His *Best American Erotic Poems* was published by Scribner's in 2008. One of his poetry collections, *Jim and Dave Defeat the Masked Man* (Soft Skull Press) was co-authored with James Cummins, who also appears in this anthology. He has also published many books in prose, the most recent of which is *A Fine Romance: Jewish Songwriters, American Songs* (Schocken, 2009). A native New Yorker, he lives there and in Ithaca, New York. He has a Ph.D. in English from Columbia University and, as a Kellett Fellow, attended Cambridge University in England.

LORI LEVY'S poems have appeared in *Poet Lore, Nimrod International Journal* and numerous other literary journals in the U.S., England, and Israel. Her health-related poems have appeared in medical and medical humanities journals, including a hybrid (poetry/prose) piece co-authored with her father, a physician. Two of her poems were published in *Psychological Perspectives.* She lives with her family in Los Angeles, but "home," she tells us, "has also been Vermont and Israel."

BETTY BONHAM Lies has taught English and creative writing for many years, working with students of all ages, from kindergarten to adults. She was named a Distinguished Teaching Artist by the New Jersey State Council on the Arts, and was twice awarded the NJ Governor's Award in Arts Education. She is a Dodge Poet for the Geraldine R. Dodge Foundation. The author of three volumes of poetry (*The Blue Laws, The Day After I Drowned* and *Padiddle*), her poems have been widely published and anthologized. A fourth, *The Cliff's Edge,* is forthcoming from Aldrich Press. She has also published three books of prose, including *Earth's Daughters: Stories of Women in Classical Mythology.*

KATE LIGHT, born in 1960, who died suddenly in 2016, had published in many leading literary magazines, including *The Paris Review, The Formalist, Sparrow, Barrow Street* and *Feminist Studies.* Her first collection, *The Laws of Falling Bodies,* was co-recipient of the 1997 Nicholas Roerich Prize. She had also been a fellow at Yaddo and at the Sewanee Writers' Conference. A resident of New York City, she was a violinist with the New York City Opera.

EUGENE MAHON, born in the West of Ireland, is a Training and Supervising Analyst at the Columbia Center for Psychoanalytic Training and Research in New York City, where he also has a private practice in adult and child psychoanalysis. A prolific writer in more than one genre, he has published many clinical articles as well as articles on Shakespeare, Coleridge and other authors. He has also published a fable, *Rensal the Redbit,* and one of his poems, "Steeds of Darkness," was set to music by the American composer Miriam Gideon.

PETER MARCUS' poems have appeared in many well-known literary magazines, including *The Antioch Review, Ploughshares, Poetry, Prairie Schooner* and more than fifty others. His work has also been anthologized in two human rights anthologies published by Lost Horse Press and is forthcoming in *Broken Atoms in Our Hands,* an anthology of poems on nuclear war/disaster (Shabda Press). He has been the recipient of a grant from the Connecticut Fellowship for the Arts and residency fellowships at Vermont Studio Center, the Marble House Project and Norton Island, and upcoming in May 2017, at PLAYA.

JAMIE MCKENDRICK, born in Liverpool, UK, now lives in Oxford, where he teaches part-time and reviews poetry and the visual arts for a number of newspapers and magazines. He is the author of six books of poetry, the most recent of which is *Out There* (2012), winner of the Hawthornden Prize. Editor of the *Faber Book of 20th Century Italian Poems,* his translations from Italian include novels and short-stories by Giorgio Bassani and a verse play by Pier Paolo Pasolino. His translation of Valerio Magrelli's *The Embrace: Selected Poems,* published in a U.S. bilingual edition as *Vanishing Points,* won the 2010 John Florio Prize for Italian translation and the 2010 Oxford-Weidenfeld Translation Prize. His translation of the poetry of Antonella Anedda, *Archipelago,* was published in 2014.

MERLE MOLOFSKY, a psychoanalyst in private practice in New York City, received the 2012 Gradiva Award for Poetry from the National Association for the Advancement of Psychoanalysis. Her novel, *Streets 1970,* was published in 2015 by IP Books, and two volumes of poetry by Poets Union Press in 2011. Her psychoanalytic publications include book chapters and journal articles. She is on the editorial board of the *Psychoanalytic Review* and on the faculty of the Psychological National Association for Psychoanalysis. She also serves on the Faculty and Advisory Board of the Harlem Family Institute.

JED MYERS lives in Seattle. His poetry collections include *Watching the Perseids,* which received the Sacramento Poetry Center Book Award; a chapbook, *The Nameless* (Finishing Line Press) and another chapbook forthcoming from Egress Studio Press. His work has received *Southern Indiana Review's* Editors' Award, the *Literal Latte* Poetry Award, *Blue Lyra Review's* Longish Poem Award and, in the UK, the McLellan Poetry Prize. He has had several poems and an essay published in *JAMA,* the journal of the American Medical Association. Many other poems have appeared or are forth-coming in journals such as *Prairie Schooner,*

Painted Bride Quarterly and others. Recently, he was Guest Poetry Editor for the journal *Bracken.*

ALICIA SUSKIN OSTRIKER, who recently moved back to New York City after many years in Princeton, New Jersey, is a major American poet and literary critic who has received numerous awards and honors for her work and has been a finalist three times for the National Book Award. She teaches in the low-residency MFA program at Drew University and is currently a chancellor of the Academy of American Poets. Her latest poetry collection is *Waiting for the Light* (University of Pittsburgh Press, 2017).

DOROTHY PARKER is another author who needs little introduction. Born in New Jersey, she grew up in New York City and became famous as a poet, short-story writer, critic and satirist. She was also a civil rights activist.

ZARA RAAB grew up in rural northern California, which she writes about in her collection, *Swimming the Eel.* Her other books include *Fracas & Asylum* (David Robert Books, 2013), *The Book of Gretel* and *Rumpelstiltskin, or What's in a Name?* a finalist for the Dana Award. Her book reviews and poems have appeared in such journals as *West Branch, Arts & Letters, Crab Orchard Review* and many others. A former contributing editor to *Poetry Flash* and *The Redwood Coast Review*, she is now settled in Western Massachusetts.

ARLENE KRAMER RICHARDS is a practicing psychoanalyst in Manhattan, where she lives with her husband, the well-known psychoanalyst Arnold Richards. She is a Training and Supervising Analyst, New York Freudian Society; a Fellow of the Institute for Psychoanalytic Training and Research, and a member of APsaA and IPA. In addition to poetry, she has written a number of children's books, including four co-authored with Irene Willis. She is also coeditor of *Fantasy, Myth and Reality:Essays in Honor of Jacob Arlow* (IUP, 1988) and co-editor, with Lucille Spira and Arthur A. Lynch, of *Encounters with Loneliness: Only the Lonely* (IP

Books, 2013). She has also written many papers on female sexuality, sexual perversion, and gambling.

ARNOLD RICHARDS, editor of *The Journal of the American Psychoanalytic Association* from 1994 to 2003 and before that of the *American Psycho-analyst,* is a Training and Supervising Analyst at the New York Psychoanalytic Institute. He is a member of the American Psychoanalytic Association and received its a Distinguished Contributor Award in 2004. Other memberships include the American Psychological Association-Division 39, the New York Pyschoanalytic Society and Institute, the New York Freudian Society, the Psychoanalytic Association of New York, the Western New York Psychoanalytic Society, Honorary Member of the American Institute of Psychoanalysis/ Karen Horney Clinic and the New Jersey Psychoanalytic Society. He is the former Chairman of the Board of the YIVO Institute for Jewish Research.

ROBIN SCOFIELD is the author of two collections, *And the Ass Saw the Angel* and *Sunfield Cantos* (Mouthfeel Press), and she has poems appearing in *The Malpais Review, The San Pedro River Review, The Texas Weather Anthology, Aster(ix)* and *Pilgrimage.* Her third collection, *Drive,* became available in 2016. She is Poetry Editor for *BorderSenses* and writes with the Tumblewords Project in El Paso, Texas, where she lives.

NANCY SCOTT has been the Managing Editor of *U.S.1 Worksheets,* the journal of the U.S.1 Poets' Cooperative in New Jersey, for more than a decade. She is also the author of nine collections of poetry, most recently of *Ah, Men* (Aldrich Press, 2016), a retrospective of the men who have influenced her life. An artist working primarily in collage and mixed media, she enjoys exhibiting and/or publishing her art and poetry together. *On Location* (March Street Press, 2011) is her book of ekphrastic poetry.

HENRY SEIDEN is a psychologist and psychoanalyst who lives and practices in Forest Hills, Queens (which, as some of you may not know, is part of New York City). In his professional role, he is a member of the

Board of Editors of *Psychoanalytic Psychology* and *Division /Review,* journals of Division 39 of the American Psychological Association. Within that role, he is co-author of *Silent Grief: Living in the Wake of Suicide* (Scribner's, 1988), which has been translated into Chinese, Portuguese and Russian. Among his professional papers, some of which overlap with his knowledge of poetry and skill as a poet, are articles on Wallace Stevens and on using poetry in psychotherapy with children. He is also Poetry Editor of *Division/Review.*

ANNE SEXTON (1928-1974) is known to poetry readers for the openly confessional, personal nature of her work, for her friendship with another famous poet, Maxine Kumin, and for her suicide. She won the Pulitzer Prize in 1967. Many of her poems deal with her psychoanalysis.

LAURA SHEAHEN'S poems have appeared in *Stirring, The Manhattan Review, Posse Review* and several journals in the UK. She works in refugee aid.

ELIZABETH ANNE SOCOLOW won the Barnard Poetry Prize in 1987 , and her manuscript, *Laughing at Gravity: Conversations with Isaac Newton,* was published by Beacon Press. Her second collection, *Between Silence and Praise,* was published by Ragged Sky Press of Princeton, New Jersey. Since then, she has published eight volumes of poetry, most recently a chapbook entitled *Rose Petals and Elephant Ears.* She has had a long teaching career, including stints as a guest poet at Barnard and at Vassar and as a poet in the schools in New Jersey. Her work has garnered many awards, including two from the New Jersey State Council on the Arts.

JILL STEIN is a psychotherapist who lives in Princeton, New Jersey. She has published two chapbooks of poems, *Cautionary Tales* (Finishing Line Press) and *Steeplechase* (Main St. Rag). Her work has also appeared in *Rattle, Poetry Northwest, Seattle Review, West Branch, MacGuffin, U.S. 1 Worksheets,* and other literary magazines. She has received three grants from the NJ State Council on the Arts and has not been a candidate for President of the U.S.

MAXINE SUSMAN has published six chapbooks, most recently *Provincelands* in 2016. Her poems also appear in *Fourth River, Ekphrasis, Blueline, Adanna, Paterson Literary Review, The Healing Muse* and elsewhere. She won third place in the 2016 Allen Ginsberg Contest and Honorable Mention for the 2017 New Jersey Poets Prize. She teaches poetry writing and short-story classes at the Osher Lifelong Learning Institute of Rutgers University, where she earned the Marlene Pomper Teaching Award. She lives in central New Jersey and performs with the Cool Women poetry ensemble.

CHRIS WATERS, of Devon, UK, is a free-lance poet/tutor/storyteller who has worked extensively across southwest England with young and adult groups and audiences. Although performance is his forte, he is equally good on the page. His poetry has won several national prizes, including the Bridport, which he won twice. He was also a finalist for the Plough Prize, Devon, and for Poetry Wivenhoe. In 2010 he was Writer-in-Residence at the Appledore Book Festival. He has two collections of poetry, both published by Mudlark Press: *Arisaig* (2010) and *Through a Glass Lately* (2014). In Autumn 2014 he was in a touring poetry performance with his old friend and fellow poet, Chris Fogg, also in this anthology.

MICHAEL WATERS' books include *The Dean of Discipline*, forthcoming in 2018 from University of Pittsburgh Press; *Celestial Joyride* (2016); *Gospel Night* (2011); *Darling Vulgarity* (2006 – finalist for the *Los Angeles Times* Book Prize and *Parthenopi: New and Selected Poems* (2001 – finalist for the Paterson Poetry Prize) from BOA Editions. He has co-edited *Contemporary American Poetry* (Houghton Mifflin, 2006) and *Perfect in Their Art: Poems on Boxing from Homer to Ali* (Southern Illinois UP, 2003). His poems have appeared in many journals, including *Poetry, American Poetry Review, Paris Review, Yale Review, Kenyon Review*, and *Rolling Stone*. Recipient of five Pushcart Prizes and fellowships from the NEA, Fulbright Foundation and NJ State Council on the Arts, he teaches at Monmouth University and in the Drew University MFA Program in Poetry & Poetry in Translation.

SUSAN WHEATLEY is an Ohio lawyer who is considered outstanding by her peers and who compares estate planning to poetry. "We're thinking into the future for that client about their own transience .... Poetry, to me at least, is a way of managing a human awareness of our transience in the world." A colleague in Cincinnati says of her, "She takes poetry very seriously, and she and I think the values that drove her to poetry also drove her to the estate planning practice: trying to understand and help people make sense of the human condition." Wheatley has served on the board of Cincinnati's Mercantile Library, where in 2004 she founded the Walnut Street Poetry Society.

IRENE WILLIS is the editor who has gathered the work of all these poets into *Climate of Opinion: Sigmund Freud in Poetry.*

Acknowledgments

Grateful acknowledgment is made to the American Psychoanalytic Foundation for their generous support of this project and to the following publications and individual poets who have given permission to use these poems. A special thank-you to James Cummins, Curator of the Elliston Poetry Collection at the University of Cincinnati, not only for letting us use his poem but for gracious help in getting contact information for some of these poets.

Akhtar, Salman: "Summary" from *Between Hours: A Collection of Poems by Psychoanalysts, Edited by Salman Akhtar* (Karnac). Reprinted by permission of the poet.

Auden, W.H.: "For Sigmund Freud" Reprinted by permission of *The Kenyon Review.*

Bates, Milton: "The Discretion of Freud's Reading Chair." Used by permission of the poet.

Berlin, Richard M.: How a Psychiatrist Writes a Poem" from *Secret Wounds* (BkMK Press) and "Transference" from *Psychiatric Times.* Used by permission of the poet.

Berry, Emily: "Freud's Beautiful Things, A Cento" and "Freud's War, A Cento" from *Poetry Magazine.* Reprinted by permission of the poet.

Blades, Maroula: "Nostalgia." Used by permission of the poet.

Blossom, Laurel: "No Is the Answer, The Answer Is No" from *The Papers Said* (Greenhouse Review Press). Reprinted by permission of the poet.

Bremner, R.: "In Paterson, at Blimpie's" from *Paterson Literary Review.* Used by permission of the poet.

Brice, Charles: "Identification." Used by permission of the poet.

Carr, Fern G.Z.: "Freudian Slip" Used by permission of the poet.

Carson, Anne: "Freud Town" from *Plainwater: Essays and Poetry by Anne Carson,* 1995. Used by permission of Alfred A. Knopf, an imprint of the Knopf

Doubleday Publishing Group, a division of Penguin Random House LLC.

Coombes, William: " A Child's Life Sentence" and "Stones in Shoes on the Shoreline of Dark Lake" Used by permission of the poet.

Cummins, James: "Freud" from *"The Antioch Review"* and *Best American Poetry.* Reprinted by permission of the poet.

Daley, Tim: "Mass for Shut-ins." Used by permission of the poet.

Derricotte, Toi: "Speculations about 'I" from *Poetry Magazine.* Reprinted by permission of the poet.

Dobyns, Stephen: "Thelonius Monk" from Garrison Keillor's *Good Poems for Hard Times.* Reprinted by permission of the poet.

Duckler, Merridawn: "Earth Room." Used by permission of the poet.

Dowd, Juditha: "Viewing Manet's Olympia with My Granddaughter." Used by permission of the poet.

Dus, Lisken Van Pelt: "And These Are My Fears" from *What We're Made Of* (Cherry Grove Collections) and "What the Computer Doesn't Know." Used by permission of the poet.

Emanuel, Lynn: "On Waking after Dreaming of Raoul" from *The Nerve of It: New and Selected Poems* (University of Pittsburgh Press). Used by permission of the poet.

Freud, Anna: "A Poem from *Wolf*" and "Thoughts of a Young Girl." Reprinted from blogger *I Love Poetry,* who says she found them while reading a biography of Freud.

Fogg, Chris: "The Waitress from Mass MoCA* (*Massachusetts Museum of Contemporary Art)" from *Special Relationships: Poems and Stories* (Mudlark Press). Reprinted by permission of the poet.

Gardner, Cynthia Read: "Accused" Used by permission of the poet.

Gerrish, Deborah: "After Ravensbruck: The Woman from Holland Speaks to Me in a Dream." Used by permission of the poet.

Giannini, David: "Freudians, Keep Out" from *Side-Ways* (Quale Press) and *Span of Thread* (Cervena Barva Press). Reprinted by permission of the poet.

Goetsch, Diana: "First Time Reading Freud" from *Best American Poetry.* Reprinted by permission of the poet.

Glück, Louise: "Humidifier" from *Averno* and "The Sword in the Stone" from *Faithful and Virtuous Night* (Farrar, Straus & Giroux). Reprinted by permission of the publisher.

H.D. (Hilda Doolittle): "The Master." Reprinted by permission of *JStor.*

Hollander, Jean: "And they shall wear purple ..." from *New and Selected Poems* (Sheep Meadow Press). Reprinted by permission of the poet.

Katsarou, Vasiliki: "Terrarium." Used by permission of the poet.

Larkin, Philip: "This Be the Verse" from *Collected Poems* edited by Anthony Thwaite (Farrar, Straus & Giroux and The Marvell Press). Reprinted by permission of the publisher.

Lefkowitz, Josh: "Mario Lopez." Used by permission of the poet.

Lehman, David: "Freud Quiz." Used by permission of the poet.

Lies, Betty Bonham: "The First Dream" from *The Day After I Drowned* (Cherry Grove Collections). Reprinted by permission of the poet.

Levy, Lori: "On Closing the Basement Door" from *Saranac Review.* Used by permission of the poet.

Light, Kate: "Your Unconscious Speaks to My Unconscious" from *The Penguin Book of the Sonnet, Edited by Phyllis Levin.* Used by permission of the Estate of Kate Light.

Mahon, Eugene: "Cloak and Dagger," "Freud," and "First Visit to Bergasse 19" all used by permission of the poet.

McKendrick, Jamie: "Freudiana." Used by permission of the poet.

Marcus, Peter: "Love Duck." Used by permission of the poet.

Molofsky, Merle: "Creative Listening." Used by permission of the poet.

Myers, Jed: "The Best Thing for It." Used by permission of the poet.

Ostriker, Alicia Suskin: "Misery and Frustration" from *No Heaven* ; "Family: Attempted Speech" and "Insomnia" from *The Book of Seventy* (All from Pittsburgh University Press and reprinted by permission of the poet.

Parker, Dorothy: "The Passionate Freudian to His Love" from *Not Much Fun: The Lost Poems of Dorothy Parker, Edited by Stuart Silverstein* (Scribner's). Now in the public domain. No permission needed.

Raab, Zara: "Fracas in the Street" from *Fracas & Asylum* (David Robert Books). Reprinted by permission of the poet.

Richards, Arlene Kramer: "Halloween." Used by permission of the poet.

Richards, Arnold: "Study Group" Used by permission of the poet.

Scofield, Robin: "The Encoder" Used by permission of the poet.

Scott, Nancy: "Into the Wild." Used by permission of the poet.

Seiden, Henry: "From an Analyst's Notebook – Case Report" Used by permission of the poet.

Sexton, Anne: "Said the Poet to the Analyst," from *The Complete Poems* (Mariner Books). Used by permission of the publisher.

Sheahen, Laura: "Minotaur." Used by permission of the poet.

Socolow, Elizabeth Anne: "Freud and the Others in the Old Days" and "They Loom Large, Parents." Used by permission of the poet.

Stein, Jill: "When I Was Six My Father Had the Power" from *Steeplechase* (Main Street Rag). Reprinted by permission of the poet.

Susman, Maxine: "Exhibit of Freud's Neurological Drawings and Diagrams of the Mind." Used by permission of the poet.

Waters, Chris: "Odysseus, His Homecoming." Used by permission of the poet.

Waters, Michael: "Sick Student" from *Celestial Joyride* (BOA Editions, Ltd.) Reprinted by permission of the publisher.

Wheatley, Susan: "The Winter Meetings of the Freudians" from *Paterson Literary Review.* Used by permission of the poet.

Willis, Irene: "Always the Man Somewhere" from *Cosmopolitan.* Reprinted by permission of the poet.

Many thanks also to three people whose technical skill and conscientiousness helped me enormously with this project:

- Ernie Lowell, Berkshire Data Solutions, Otis, MA
- Luann Jette, Arnell Office Services, Southampton, MA and
- Marcia Mayper, Innovative Computing, New Lebanon, NY

CPSIA information can be obtained
at www.ICGtesting.com
Printed in the USA
LVHW03s1630050918
589229LV00016B/1035/P